W9-CMS-469

Letters to Contemplatives

Letters to Contemplatives

William Johnston

ORBIS BOOKS
Maryknoll, New York 10545

248.4
JOL

The Catholic Foreign Mission Society of America (Maryknoll) recruits and
trains people for overseas missionary service. Through Orbis Books, Maryknoll
aims to foster the international dialogue that is essential to mission. The books
published, however, reflect the opinions of their authors and are not meant to
represent the official position of the society.

Copyright © 1991 by William Johnston
First published in Great Britain by Fount Paperbacks, an imprint of Harper-
Collins Religious, 77-85 Fulham Palace Road, London W6 8JB
Published in the United States of America by Orbis Books, Maryknoll, NY 10545
Typeset in Great Britain, printed in the United States of America
248.4
All rights reserved

ORBIS/ISBN 0-88344-784-3

For the Brethren
in
Milltown

Contents

Preface

These letters were written during a sabbatical which brought me from Tokyo to Manila and on to California. After spending some months at the University of Santa Clara I went to Ireland for six months. Then I returned to Japan via Hong Kong. Let me say a word about the people to whom these letters are addressed.

Frank and Betty, husband and wife, are both university lecturers who plan to spend a year of study in Japan. Frank is interested in Zen and in dialogue with Buddhism. Though he is a fine scholar, his interest in Buddhism is not just academic. He has a deep interior life and through dialogue with other religions he is searching for contemplation.

Betty is less interested in Buddhism. Her uncle, whom she loved and revered, was a missionary in China and spent some years in a communist gaol before being expelled to the Philippines where he died. Betty is wary about Buddhist influence on Christianity, and she wonders if the missionary zeal that fired her uncle is on the wane in the post-Vatican Church.

Maria is happily married, the mother of four children. As a college student she thought of becoming a Carmelite; but then she met David. And that was that. But her love for Carmel has not died and she longs for a contemplative life.

Ayako lives in Japan. She is a journalist and writes on religious affairs for a high-class Japanese magazine. She is interested in religion everywhere and keeps an eye on developments in China as well as in the Islamic world. Her interest is not merely journalistic. She is deeply committed to Jesus Christ and to the Gospel, and her contemplative life grows daily.

Jack is a Catholic priest with all the virtues and all the questions of the modern young priest. He loves the saying of Irenaeus that the glory of God is man and woman fully alive. He prays constantly with the determination to integrate into that prayer life his intimate relationships with other men and women. He believes in celibacy and he believes in friendship; and he has no doubt that according to the Gospel these two can be beautifully harmonized through contemplation.

Robert is an older man. His wife died more than ten years ago and his children are scattered all over the globe. He lives alone, devoting many hours to prayer and to the St Vincent de Paul Society. Outwardly he seems very successful and cheerful; but he has suffered a lot in the dark night of the soul. He knows the meaning of the void, the emptiness, the nothingness. He is a consummate mystic.

Brian is Irish American. His grandparents came from the so-called old sod and he has gone to Ireland several times to study his family tree. He has inherited a good deal of anger from his ancestors and though he is totally dedicated to peace and justice he tends to have a certain gut sympathy with the IRA. But his love for the Gospel is very real, much deeper than any anger that lurks in his unconscious mind.

All of these people are drawn to contemplation. I have no doubt that the Spirit is working powerfully in their lives as he is working in the whole human family today. I hope that my letters will be of interest to other contemplatives and non-contemplatives who wish to read them.

Sophia University
Tokyo
August 1990

Letters to Contemplatives

Dear Frank,

Many thanks for your letter which I read with great interest. So you feel drawn to Buddhism! And you would like to spend your sabbatical in Japan studying and practising Zen. Truth to tell, I get many letters like yours and usually I don't know how to answer. Anyhow, please come, if that's what you want to do. But don't blame me if you get disappointed. There is a certain amount of confusion here — as many opinions as there are people. But it is good confusion, holy confusion, pious confusion. And from the spiritual and intellectual chaos something very powerful is emerging.

As you know, we are part of something bigger, part of a great inter-religious dialogue that has spread throughout the world evoking stimulating meetings and provocative symposia everywhere — from Hawaii to Cologne and from Berkeley to Bangkok. Practitioners and scholars come together in a congenial and meditative atmosphere wherein Meister Eckhart meets Zen Master Dogen, Ramana Maharshi meets St John of the Cross, and (most important of all) the Gospel meets the *dharma*. Where all this will lead I do not know. I believe, however, that we are witnessing a spiritual revolution of great magnitude in the whole world.

I myself approach Buddhism from the standpoint of rigorous dialogue. In other words I put my roots more and more deeply in the Bible and the Christian tradition while remaining open to the *dharma* and wisdom of eastern teachers. And at the same time I wish to share the treasures of the Gospel with anyone who is willing to listen.

And in all this I see a very exciting development: *the rise of a new school of mysticism within Christianity*. Slowly but surely a new mystical contemplation is coming to birth. It is different from the medieval Christian mysticism that I learned as a novice; and it is different from traditional Buddhist or Hindu mysticism. It is a third way, a *tertium quid*. It is growing year by year.

1

Lest this prove offensive to your pious ears, let me remind you that a new mysticism is no anomaly within a developing Christianity.

The most basic and important mysticism is that of Jesus himself, followed by that of John and Paul. Indeed the whole New Testament is a storehouse of mystical lore, drawing the reader to higher consciousness. But when Christianity met neoplatonism something new was born. Under the dynamic influence of the Spirit of God there arose the so-called apophatic school of dark mysticism that comes to us powerfully in the writings of St Gregory of Nyssa, in the famous *Mystical Theology* of the pseudo-Dionysius, and in the lives and writings of enlightened mystics of the Western world. I don't need to tell you about Eckhart, Tauler, Suso, the author of *The Cloud*, St John of the Cross, St Thérèse of Lisieux and the rest. This mysticism of the dark nights continues to inspire the lives of thousands throughout the world. It will never die.

Side by side with this are other schools of mysticism associated with the great religious orders whose founders were sublimely enlightened men and women. Benedictine, Franciscan, Dominican, Jesuit, Carmelite mysticism — all rooted in the Gospel — have their distinctive flavour, their distinctive symbols and their distinctive language.

And today, I say, another school of mysticism is coming to birth, thanks to an ongoing dialogue with Buddhism, Taoism and Hinduism. Christians who have met these religions know how profoundly mystical they are — know how they stress meditation, teach a path of liberation, lead to transformation and enlightenment. We know that these powerful religions have given birth to some of the world's holiest men and women. And Christian encounter with them has already generated a new and provocative movement associated with the distinguished names of Abhishiktananda in India, Enomiya-Lassalle in Japan, and Thomas Merton in America. These are the pioneers. And since their time, men and women from all arts and parts have joined in the search. I myself try modestly to follow in the footsteps of these spiritual giants, hoping to devote my remanining days (be they many or be they few, be they here or be they there) to this new mysticism. And you, too, if you would like to join the quest come and see what is happening.

But a word of caution. Do not think you are choosing a primrose path of dalliance. Far from it. There is no mysticism without renunciation: no mysticism without the cross. So sit down and count the cost, whether you have enough to build the tower, lest people mock you and say: 'This man began to build and was not able to finish.''

I will tentatively outline five characteristics of this new mysticism.

First of all, whereas traditional Christian mystical teaching has been geared to monks and nuns and professionally religious people, the new mysticism appeals also to the laity. The gurus and teachers, it is true, are still celibate and consecrated religious; but the people at large — the proverbial butcher and baker and candlestick maker — are opening their eyes and ears to the message and embarking courageously on the road to enlightenment. Now we see that contemplation is not the preserve of a few but open to all and sundry. Perhaps the old theologians who spoke of the universal vocation to mysticism are at last being vindicated. Perhaps Karl Rahner was right when he said that the fervent Christian of the future will be a mystic. Or is it that the invited guests did not show up, so the master went into the highways and byways and compelled everybody to enter into the marriage feast?

Secondly, this new mysticism speaks a different language.

Basically, it is true, all Christian mystics talk the language of the Bible. They overflow with sayings from Paul and John and the psalms and the *Song of Songs*. However, when one comes to mystical theology there can be considerable diversity in the way of speaking. Western mystical treatises from the fourteenth century used the language and the framework of Aristotle and Thomas. Scholasticism was the language of the day. And spiritual writers until the Second Vatican Council spoke of sense and spirit, of the three powers of the soul, of the memory, the understanding and the will. They catalogued virtues and vices in the manner of Aristotle's *Nichomachean Ethics* or they spoke of the seven deadly sins and their contrary virtues. They talked about union with God in scholastic terms.

The new mystical theology, on the other hand, is holistic. While it does not reject Aristotle and Thomas it appeals to psychologists like Jung and thinkers like Teilhard. It distinguishes between the ego and the self, or between the small self and the big self — it

3

is indeed filled with awe and wonder not only at the mystery of God but also at the mystery of the self. Realizing that the human person is multi-dimensional it speaks in terms of consciousness: layers of consciousness, growth in consciousness, evolution of consciousness, transformation of consciousness, higher consciousness, cosmic consciousness and the Christ consciousness. It asks if, while speaking of sense and spirit, body and soul, we could describe mystical experience more satisfactorily by speaking also of the gross body, the subtle body and the spiritual body. Believing that we cannot understand mysticism without referring to energy, it looks to Chinese medicine which speaks of the flow of energy through meridieans and of balancing the yin and the yang. Or it appeals to yoga which speaks of prana and that virulent and frightening energy called *kundalini*. And will all this help us to speak more meaningfully about love, the energy which is the core and centre of all mystical contemplation and of all true Christian living? These are questions that confront us as we grope for a new mystical theology.

And that brings me to a third characteristic of the new mysticism: emphasis on posture and breathing.

Assuredly prayer through posture and breathing is no stranger to the West. It is particularly evident in the Hesychast tradition wherein one recites the Jesus prayer to the rhythm of breathing. Nevertheless in yoga as in Buddhist meditation and, indeed, in the whole Sino-Japanese culture, posture and breathing assumed an importance undreamt of west of Suez. When Westerners come to Japan I always advise them to learn abdominal breathing. For breathing is the gateway to the unconscious and can unleash a flow of energy that leads to enlightenment. And then there is the practice of *mindfulness*, the glory of Buddhist meditation. 'When I breathe I know that I am breathing. When I walk I know that I am walking. When I sit I know that I am sitting.' Then there is the art of coming to one-pointedness by keeping the back straight, gathering strength in the lower abdomen and reciting the mantra. All these ways (I prefer to say ways rather than techniques) lead people to the door of the interior castle. But remember, Frank, that to enter and meet the Inner Guest is the work of Grace alone.

A fourth characteristic of the new mysticism is its emphasis on faith.

Needless to say, all prayer and mysticism are based on radical faith; but here I speak of a faith that is divorced from words and letters and thought. We call this pure faith, naked faith, dark faith.

I have been astonished by the totality of the Buddhist faith commitment. 'Even if it kills me, I will go through' cries the Zen practitioner. And then the radical surrender chanted at the commencement of each day's sitting: 'I put my faith in the Buddha: I put my faith in the *dharma*: I put my faith in the *sangha*.' If you were to ask a fervent Zen Buddhist: 'But why do you put your faith in the Buddha, the *dharma* and the *sangha*?' he or she would undoubtedly give no reason. She believes because she believes. She sits because she sits. And this refusal to think is carried into the very heart of Buddhist practice. In meditation one refuses to reason; one renounces all thought; one gives up all dependence on words and letters. And what happens? One enters the void. One becomes nothing. Nothing, nothing, nothing. Mu, mu, mu. This nothingness is in fact pure faith, naked faith, dark faith.

And we Christians have much to learn from Buddhist faith. It is so difficult for us (particularly for us Western Christians or Western-educated Christians) to renounce thought so as to fall into the void of pure faith. We give reasons, reasons, reasons, as though we could *prove* the doctrines of faith. But faith cannot be proved, as Kirkegaard knew so well when he spoke of the leap. And the time comes in the contemplative life when we are called to give up thinking and reasoning and discursive meditating in order to fall into the void where we believe in God for God, just as we hope in God for God and love God for God. Blessed are those who have not seen but believe. Blessed are those who have no reasons but believe.

Needless to say, this prayer of the void is highlighted in St John of the Cross and the whole tradition for which he speaks. It is not new. Nevertheless, dialogue with Buddhism can inspire us to let go of all things — of all reasoning, all thinking, all feeling — in order to fall into the void of pure faith. Just as the fervent Buddhist has this radical and naked faith in the Buddha, the *dharma* and the *sangha*, so we can have a radical and naked faith in Jesus, in the Gospel and in the Church. 'Nothing, nothing, nothing and even on the mountain nothing.' Enomiya-Lassalle used to say with a laugh: 'I teach people not to think.' And what a teacher he was!

5

A fifth characteristic of the new mysticism is emphasis on enlightenment.

After his visit to Dharmsala in North India, Merton playfully remarked that the Dalai Lama had asked whether the monk's vows were just a promise to stick around for life or whether they were leading somewhere. Obviously the Dalai Lama thought (and Merton agreed) that the vows should lead somewhere — to mystical experiences or enlightenment or whatever — just as Buddhist meditation leads to enlightenment and finally to the supreme enlightenment which is nirvana. So often Christian contemplatives do not know where they are going! But St John of the Cross knew very well. His goal was the vision of God; his suffering was the sad human condition which prevented him from seeing God face to face. 'Reveal thy presence', he cries, 'and may the vision of thy beauty be my death.' Remember that the Spanish mystic was a poet and an artist, intoxicated by beauty, longing to see the inexhaustible source of all beauty and goodness. He knew that the dazzling beauty of God would kill him but what matter? Such a death would be the gateway to eternal life where, he says, 'I shall see You in Your beauty, and You shall see me in Your beauty, and my beauty will be Your beauty and Your beauty my beauty . . . and we shall behold each other in Your beauty.' Put in cold, theological language his goal was the beatific vision.

But can he see God in this life? Yes, even in this valley of tears he has glimpses, albeit imperfect, of the stunning beauty of God; but these glimpses leave him dissatisfied and frustrated so that he cries out 'Henceforth send me no more messengers; they cannot tell me what I want to know.' It is as though he were to say, 'I want you alone: messengers, people and things who talk about you are not enough.'

Truly they are not enough but they are something. And so in this earthly life the mystics speak about a high and lofty wisdom — *sophia* or *sapientia* — which is the fruit of love and the gift of the Spirit. And within this wonderful wisdom are enlightenments, awakenings, gifts of a God who momentarily reveals His ineffable beauty and goodness and the secrets of His love.

And so if you ask with the Dalai Lama where Christian contemplation is going, I answer that it is going towards an ever deepening wisdom, to an ever growing enlightenment, to a joy that no one can take from us and which culminates in the vision of God. 'For now we see in a mirror dimly, but then face to face' (1 Corinthians 13:12)

But let me descend from the sublime to the practical. I suggest that you read *The Cloud of Unknowing* and *The Book of Privy Counselling* and (if I may say it modestly) my own *Being in Love*. St John of the Cross, of course, is a classic among classics and, in my opinion, the Spanish saint is the prince of mystics. But he is difficult at first, very difficult. Begin with his great poem, *The Spiritual Canticle*, reading the poetry and the commentary together. Yes, Merton is good, and Dr Suzuki is good, if long-winded.

Later I will recommend Buddhist texts both modern and ancient. At first, however, I advise you to read mainly Christian books. My reason? For authentic dialogue you must first be rooted and grounded in Christ and the Gospel. Only then will you be able to open your heart to all that is good in Buddhism and Hinduism. If you plunge immediately and radically into Buddhist meditation you may find yourself culturally and religiously uprooted with undesirable, if not disastrous, consequences. If you don't believe me, read the astute psychologist Jung on Zen and on yoga. I quote him liberally in my book *The Mirror Mind*. Jung loved and admired Zen and yoga but urged Western people to approach them with caution. It is particularly hazardous to get involved in the whole area of energy — *ki, prana, kundalini* — without a grounding in Christian contemplative love.

But more important than reading is sitting — sitting cross-legged for at least twenty minutes each day, reciting the Jesus prayer or some other mantra or practising centring prayer or entering the cloud.

Is Betty interested in meditation? If so, you can sit together. I know a couple who sit together with great fruit. They claim that silent meditation, which is a kind of wordless dialogue, has opened up a whole new dimension in their relationship.

And be prepared for shock!

Foreigners here talk, sometimes ruefully, about culture shock. On the surface Tokyo looks like New York or London; but underneath lies a different world, a different consciousness, a different mind-set. Japan has been moulded by centuries of

Buddhism, Taoism, Confucianism, without losing its distinctively Japanese identity. Reactions are quite different from those of the West. Even businessmen need education on how to do business in Japan. So be prepared!

And then the economic shock — the shock to your wallet! The cost of living is sky high. A cup of coffee costs the equivalent of two or three dollars. But if you avoid the big hotels (yes, avoid them like the plague) you can get a bowl of rice and fish that will keep you in good health and you won't go broke. Anyhow, don't be anxious about money: tomorrow will look after itself.

Let me know when you plan to come. I'm soon leaving Tokyo for a sabbatical in the U S and Ireland; but I'll be back next year before you arrive. I'd love to meet you at Narita airport.

Greetings to Betty and the children. May God bless you all!

Bill J———— S. J.

Tokyo
2 February 1989

Dear Frank,

I write this letter in a coffee shop in downtown Tokyo. I love these coffee shops with their classical music and quiet atmosphere. The Japanese are masters of atmosphere (what contemplative silence hovers over the temples in Kyoto!) and I sometimes escape to a tasteful coffee shop to write letters or to talk confidentially with a friend. The trouble is that the lighting is rather dim and I wonder how long my poor eyes will stand the strain. Anyhow, I have just re-read your last letter which I enjoyed a lot.

You ask about the possibility of a 'Christian Zen.' Well, some people use that terminology and at one time I used it myself. Some of my colleagues, distinguishing between Zen and Zen Buddhism, claim that Zen — i.e., the imageless meditation, can be extracted from its Buddhist background and incarnated into Christianity. And in this way they have a Christian Zen — just as one could have a Jewish Zen or a Muslim Zen or whatever.

I have abandoned this approach. It is true that I have written a book entitled *Christian Zen*; and I still stand by what I wrote there. But I no longer use that terminology. I make no claims to practise Zen. I prefer honest-to-God dialogue. Standing firmly on the Christian tradition and opening my mind and heart to all that is good in Zen or in yoga or in Tibetan mysticism, I search for a new Christian mysticism which will be a third way.

But let me get to your main question. You say you are greatly attracted by this new mysticism. You think it is all very fascinating. But you are still uncertain about the role of Jesus. Sitting and breathing and practising awareness or mindfulness — these are wonderful and invigorating exercises. But what about Jesus of Nazareth to whom we make our basic commitment? Where does He fit in?

Good question, Frank! I congratulate you on your prudence, insight and perspicacity.

And let me first assure you that you must never enter into the

9

path of meditation without a total commitment to Jesus and the Gospel. On this point you must make no compromise. And you will find, as I find, that the commitment remains deep in your consciousness even when you are not thinking explicitly of Jesus or reflecting on His words and actions. The human mind is very, very profound, and in prayer the hidden layers are always at work. It is there that your commitment to Jesus lies.

Having said this, however, it is also true that you point to an important problem that has preoccupied mystical theologians for many centuries. There have always been would-be mystics who, aspiring to a silent and imageless prayer of pure spirit, have thought that they must abandon the humanity of Jesus. Their great opponent was St Teresa of Avila who claims that she herself did for a time abandon the humanity of Jesus, only to discover that it was an act of high treason. 'Is it possible, Lord', she writes, 'that for so much as an hour I should have entertained the thought that thou couldn't hinder my greatest good?'

But the tendency to escape from the Incarnation in order to contemplate the divine essence in all its spirituality persists. It runs contrary to the whole Christian tradition. In particular it goes against the Councils of Ephesus and Chalcedon which declared that the divinity of Jesus cannot be separated from his humanity. And the Holy Office in 1687, coming down like a ton of bricks on the hapless Miguel de Molinos, condemned the proposition: 'There can be no perfect contemplation, save only of the divinity.' Today, the problem is more alive than ever and I am glad that you are confronting it. Let me say a few Christological words that may be helpful.

Much depends on what we mean by the humanity of Jesus; for the human person, including the person of Jesus, is very, very mysterious. We can think of the man Jesus who worked as a carpenter, climbed the mountain, walked by the sea of Galilee and ate with his friends. This Jesus is real. We can also think of the Jesus who rose from the dead, ascended into heaven, entered into his glory and will be with us always, to the close of the age. This Jesus is also real. The old authors said that before the resurrection the divinity hides itself: after the resurrection the divinity shines forth.

10

Let me add a few more words of Christology. From the beginning of the twentieth century, scripture scholarship, using the historical critical method, has concentrated on the historical Jesus, going behind the New Testament words in search of the mysterious Galilean, trying to discover the very words that issued from his lips. This approach has been of immense value since it confirms our Christian belief that the word was made flesh in a specific place and at a specific time. But if we limit ourselves to such historical research we are in danger of missing the whole point.

For the whole point of the New Testament is that Jesus is alive. The early disciples went out into the Mediterranean world; and their message was: 'This Jesus who was crucified has risen from the dead. He is alive and he will be with us always even to the close of the age.' And if someone asked: 'But how do you know he is alive?' they responded: 'We saw him.' Paul tells us clearly that Jesus appeared to Cephas, then to the twelve. 'Then he appeared to James, then to all the apostles. Last of all, as to one untimely born, he appeared also to me' (1Corinthians 15:7). And the evangelists, when they write about Jesus asleep in the boat or preaching on the mount or giving bread to the multitude, are always conscious that the same Jesus has entered into his glory, and sits at the right hand of the Father. 'Was it not necessary that the Christ should suffer these things and enter into His glory?' (Luke 24:26). Jesus is alive.

And the message of Christianity today is the same. Jesus is alive. If someone asks: 'But how do you know he is alive?', we cannot answer that we have seen him as these first disciples saw him; but we can say we have met him in faith. And if the questioner goes on: 'But where is he?', we can answer that he is present when we call on his name; he is present in our neighbour, particularly in the poor and sick and oppressed; he is present in the sacraments, particularly in the Eucharist. He is with us always, even to the close of the age.

But what kind of body does He have?

Asked about the bodies of those who rise from the dead, Paul answers almost rudely: 'You foolish man!' (1 Corinthians 15:36) as if to say, 'Don't ask foolish questions!' There are all kinds of bodies; and the risen or glorified body is quite unimaginable. 'For not all flesh is alike, but there is one kind for man, another for animals, another for birds, and another for fish. There are celestial

11

bodies and there are terrestrial bodies . . . '(1 Corinthians 15:39). Here we are faced with mystery. We can have no adequate image of the glorified body of Jesus.

One thing, however, we can say. The glorified body is outside space and time. Hence we can talk about the cosmic Christ or the Christ of the universe. This is Jesus who is the Alpha and the Omega, the beginning and the end. This is the Jesus in whom all things were created. This is the Jesus who being lifted up from the Earth will draw all things to himself. 'The Word became flesh and dwelt amongst us' (John 1:14). For those who meditate it is particularly important to remember that Jesus is within us, both as individuals and as a community. Paul's cry: 'I live now not I but Christ lives in me' (Galatians 2:20), is a favourite text of the mystics. And then in the fourth gospel we read of the vine and the branches and hear the astounding words of Jesus: 'He who eats my flesh and drinks my blood abides in me and I in him' (John 6:56). And doesn't the seventeenth chapter end with the remarkable prayer 'that the love with which Thou hast loved me may be in them and I in them' (John 17:26).

Jesus within! How moving is the prayer of Augustine: 'Late have I loved you, oh Beauty ever ancient, ever new, late have I loved you! You were within me but I was outside . . . you were within me but I was not with you.' And the Eucharistic Jesus! Augustine heard a voice: 'I am the food of grown man; grow then and you will feed on Me. Nor will you change me into yourself like bodily food, but you will be changed into me.' And then St Leo the Great, quoted in the Council, tells us succinctly that 'The partaking of the Body and Blood of Christ does nothing other than transform us into that which we consume.' The implications of this patristic teaching are enormous; but I cannot go into them here.

All this is of the greatest importance for would-be contemplatives. Some naïve souls, alas, think their prayer is not Christo-centric unless they make a composition of place and form a mental picture of Jesus. Let them read Paul and John! Let them read Augustine! If you practise mindfulness or *vipassana* or awareness of breathing or silent non-objective prayer, do not think you must entertain a picture of Jesus. Indeed you need not objectify him at all; for he is there dwelling secretly in the depth of your consciousness; and

12

all imageless though He is, he is your intimate friend and your tender lover.

But when you practise non-objective contemplation it is very, very desirable that you receive the Eucharist, if possible, daily. 'He who eats my flesh and drinks my blood abides in me, and I in him' (John 6:56). The great Enomiya Lassalle, our pioneer in the practice of Zen, always took time to celebrate the Eucharist quietly in the Buddhist temples where for days and days he sat doggedly in the lotus.

And practice of this non-objective contemplation will enable you to put on the Christ consciousness in accordance with those Pauline words: 'Let this mind be in you which was in Christ Jesus' (Philippians 2:5). As you do this you will discover that you go out to all the world with a truly ecstatic love. Yes, your consciousness will expand in love for all human beings who have ever been or ever will be, for friend and foe alike, for the trees and the plants, the ocean and the atmosphere, for the whole garden of the universe which we, poor humans, have treated with such abominable ruthlessness. For Jesus within is now loving all creation and the source of all creation, his eternal Father. Abba, Father!

Many Christological difficulties arise from a misunderstanding of what mystics call the void. Let me explain.

When one enters the deeper layers of contemplative prayer one sooner or later experiences the void, the emptiness, the nothingness, the darkness, the unknowing, the profound mystical silence. All these words point to the same reality. Yes, it is as though there is within me an immense and bottomless void. And when one first experiences this void there is an absence of thought and imaginative pictures, and perhaps there is a certain forgetfulness, as forms are buried beneath a cloud of forgetting. 'Nothing, nothing, nothing, and even on the mountain nothing.' But the nothing is all; the emptiness is fullness, the void is plenitude. To experience the vast inner nothing is to experience the vast inner all. It is to experience the 'eternal now'. This is the doctrine of St John of the Cross and the whole apophatic tradition which he represents.

Now you will find that the void plays a vital role also in Buddhist experience. In Zen monasteries throughout Japan you will hear Buddhists chanting the hauntingly beautiful *Heart Sutra* which is a hymn to *mu* or *ku* or the void. It is a poem of thanksgiving to emptiness — for there are no eyes, no ears, no suffering, no enlightenment . . . nothing! It is precisely the chanting of this sutra, followed by prolonged sitting in zazen, that carries the fervent Buddhist into the void.

And the *Heart Sutra* is full of paradox. One paradox of crucial import runs :

Form is emptiness
And emptiness is form

This comes as a shock because form and emptiness are opposites. How can form be emptiness and emptiness form?

Yet this is true to experience. Let me be personal. At rush hour I have stood in the hurly-burly of Shinjuku with the traffic swirling around and the noise at its peak, with people laughing and talking or rushing to their destinations, with street artists displaying their paintings, with saffron-robed Hare-Krishna devotees chanting their hymns and distributing their literature. Life is fast in Shinjuku. And I have stood there experiencing the immense inner void and at the same time acutely aware of the forms around me. I can hear all the noise of Shinjuku; and beneath it all I 'hear' the immense void at the centre of my being — at the deep heart's core. This is the eternal now. And I know without any doubt that form is emptiness and emptiness is form.

As this emptiness deepens, one carries it around always — when one is talking and laughing and teaching and walking and standing on the train. It is there when one goes to sleep at night and when one awakens in the morning. At first the void is frightening, terribly frightening, as one loses all security; but later it becomes a spring of clear water welling up to life eternal and giving great joy. This is because one comes to realize that the void has a source: and the source is Jesus, the Word Incarnate, the Inner Guest. And he is opening up the way to an even more immense and limitless and bottomless void which is the Father.

Now the point I want to make is that the void is not total oblivion. It does not mean that one wipes out all forms and becomes a blank. Forms are present. For form is emptiness and emptiness is form. *What constitutes the void is not absence of thought or absence of image but detachment.* You experience the void when you let go, let go, let go. This is the key. No clinging, no grasping.

14

And so when this void deepens and grows and develops, you may find that Jesus and Mary are present: you can dialogue with them, and read the Gospel, and meditate freely on the passion. I am quite sure that St Teresa did just that — as also did mystics like Padre Pio. They were deeply, deeply in the void and at the same time they were with Jesus *in Gethsemane or with Jesus going to Emmaus*. As one grows in maturity, there is no tension between the void and the mysteries of the earthly life of Jesus. The great insight of St Teresa of Avila was just that.

Moreover, the void, far from being pure negation, is intensely creative. Great art and great poetry come out of the void. I have no doubt that the rich and sensuous *Anima Christi* ('blood of Christ inebriate me') welled up from the void; and the exquisite poetry of St John of the Cross arose from the immense, inner nothingness that he experienced in prison as in prayer. And the *Spiritual Exercises* came from the void of silence and mysticism that Ignatius experienced in Manresa.

For the void is a bottomless well of love. At first it does not seem like love. You are the log soaked in water; and the fire of love is engaged in burning out the smoke or the dirt. But when this smoke clears away the log catches fire and becomes a living flame of love.

But let me return to Buddhism. You know that Buddhist teaching distinguishes between *Nirvana* and *Samsara*. *Nirvana* is the ultimate void, the blowing out of the candle, the absolute nothingness. *Samsara*, on the other hand, is the cycle of birth and death, the coming and going, the hustle and bustle of life lived in the midst of earthly passion. What different worlds, you might say, are *Nirvana* and *Samsara*! But no, no, no! Buddhist doctrine and, more importantly, Buddhist experience tells us that at the end *Samsara* equals *Nirvana*. That is it! Form is emptiness and emptiness is form.

St John of the Cross is accused of negativity by people who don't know what he is talking about. And Buddhism is called life-denying by Westerners who have never relished the void. Love the void; surrender to the void; for in it you will find peace, joy, creativity, love and goodness.

I'm still preparing for my sabbatical. It's always something of a wrench to leave Tokyo; but I look forward to the wide-open spaces of California.

Be sure to give my greetings to Betty and the children. Keep sitting and open your mind and heart to the void!

God's blessing on you all.

Bill J——— S. J.

PS   Last time I visited the Carmelite monastery in Reno, I found in the chapel a series of exquisite paintings drawn by one of the sisters who is an artist. One of them depicts two women, one working and the other sitting pensively on the ground. Just that. I was told that the women were Martha and Mary. And my first astonished reaction was: 'Where is Jesus?' And then I saw it. Of course. Jesus is within. Mary is the great contemplative.

Dear Betty,

Many thanks for your letter. I was delighted to hear that you are coming to Japan with Frank. Never mind that you are not interested in Zen. There are lots of other things you can learn; for Japan has a fantastic culture. You can practise the tea-ceremony or the flower arrangement or calligraphy. Or, if you prefer the martial arts, there is *aikido*. I don't recommend *karate*: it's a bit too violent for a gentle lady like you (smile). But you might like archery. All these *ways* (*do* In Japanese and *tao* in Chinese) have one thing in common: they emphasize correct breathing and they lead to one-pointedness. So learn to breathe; learn one-pointedness and let the energy (the *ki* or *chi*) flow through your body and make you fully alive. There are levels of energy and the deepest level is love. But when we talk about love we are already in the realm of religion.

But let me come to your letter. I smiled at some of your remarks. You ask if, with all this dialogue talk, evangelization and missionary zeal have gone out the window. And why preach the Gospel to people who can equally well be saved as Buddhists or Hindus? Good questions! Many people are asking them these days. Why preach the Gospel?

Listen to Paul. 'For necessity is laid on me. Woe to me if I do not preach the Gospel' (1 Corinthians 9:16). Note that Paul here gives no reasons. He is talking as a mystic and a lover, as one who feels a deep interior compulsion that cannot be denied. He could not not preach the Gospel. He must obey the inner voice. He must follow his bliss. He would fall to pieces if he did not preach the Gospel. And so he traversed the Mediterranean world, travelling to Rome and beyond, proclaiming that Jesus Christ is Lord to the glory of God the Father. 'Woe to me if I do not preach the Gospel.'

And the words of Paul echo down the corridors of time. They will never fall into oblivion. 'For necessity is laid on me. Woe to me if I do not preach the Gospel.' In this Pauline sense the Christian missionary thirst will last until the close of the age.

17

For the fact is that Paul was foolishly in love with Christ and foolishly in love with the Gospel. 'I decided to know nothing among you except Jesus Christ and Him crucified' (1 Corinthians.2:2). And he had a real love for people. His missionary zeal was simply a passionate fidelity to the greatest commandments: to love God with one's whole heart and soul and mind and strength, and to love the neighbour as one's self. This love made him become the slave of all that he might win all. To the Jews he became a Jew; to the gentiles he became a gentile; to the weak he became weak. 'I have become all things to all, that I might by all means save some. I do it all for the sake of the Gospel, that I may share in its blessings' (1 Corinthians 9: 22, 23).

And Paul's woe-to-me-if-I-do-not-preach-the-Gospel together with the Gospel command of Jesus himself gave birth to the whole evangelical thrust of Christianity. Of particular importance for me and for you is that cycle of missionary endeavour which began on 7 April 1541 when Francis Xavier, fired with the spirit of Ignatius and *The Exercises*, set sail from Lisbon for the so-called Indies. The spirit of Xavier was passed on from generation to generation to men and women who burned with missionary zeal. And last of all, as to one untimely born, his cloak fell upon me — and my companions. In the 1950s, with hearts aflame, we joyfully went East to Hong Kong and Tokyo.

The successors of Xavier were valiant and heroic men and women. Their unshakeable faith, their indomitable courage, their unquenchable zeal implanted a faith which centuries of suffering and persecution could not eradicate. Today in Goa, in Macau, in Nagasaki, in the Philippines, children of the first neophytes can be seen celebrating the Eucharist, reciting the rosary, struggling for peace and justice, proclaiming the Gospel.

And yet it is clear that today, as the twentieth century draws to a close, that magnificent cycle of missionary endeavour has come to an end. It is not that Paul's woe-to-me has been forgotten. It is not that the Lord's injunction to preach the Gospel to every creature is now invalid. It is simply that that particular expression of missionary zeal is over. The historical process has killed it. And who can fight against the inevitability of history? Or, if I would be more theologically exact, who can fight against Divine Providence working through history?

18

For the foreign missionaries in Asia have fulfilled their task, their job is done. The local churches are established with indigenous bishops and pastors and priests and sisters. Asian theologians are speaking out self-confidently, no longer looking to Europe and America for inspiration and guidance. Inculturation in liturgy and all forms of activity is on the up-and-up. In the churches you will find bustling congregations, singing and participating with a vitality seldom found in the West. Small wonder if some of the old missionaries wake up one morning to find that they are redundant, that their time has come to bow out — or to move to green fields and pastures new. This is a source of pain and acute suffering. But it is inevitable — especially as it becomes increasingly clear that the tired and aging post-Christian West can no longer send young idealistic missionaries to evangelize the world.

And there are other reasons why this cycle of missionary endeavour that began with Xavier should come to an end.

We are acutely conscious of the defects of these heroic missionaries, even when we acknowledge that these defects stemmed principally from historical and cultural conditioning.

One great drawback was their theology. For in the West there arose a pernicious theology of *outside the church no salvation* and of the *massa damnata* condemned to eternal fire because they were not baptized. And this was to influence the whole missionary effort. Xavier himself, educated at the University of Paris and convinced that thousands, indeed millions, were going to hell because they were not baptized, travelled through Asia baptizing and baptizing until his arm fell helplessly to his side from sheer exhaustion. Other missionaries felt they could do no greater service to the peoples they encountered than to go into the highways and the byways and *compel* them to enter the marriage feast. After all is it not lawful to use any means — rice or fire or the sword or political skulduggery — to save people from such a dire fate?

But let us not exaggerate. Let us be fair. Paul's woe-to-me-if-I-do-not-preach-the-Gospel never died: it was fully alive in the hearts of many. Take Xavier himself. I cannot believe that he was motivated solely by a theology of the *massa damnata*. He was too big a man for that. Like Paul he was a mystic and a lover. He composed a wonderful prayer: 'My God I love you not because

19

. . . ', as if to say that he loved God not from fear of hell or hope of heaven but because Jesus loved him and embraced him from the cross. And so Xavier was motivated principally by love. 'For necessity is laid on me. Woe to me if I do not preach the Gospel.'

A second defect of the old missionaries was, from our viewpoint, a woeful ignorance of anthropology. They could not distinguish between the Gospel and Western culture, nor could they appreciate the indigenous cultures with which they came in contact. Many thought they could best serve the people by educating them in Western languages, teaching them to use knives and forks, treating them to a Western cuisine, giving them Western names, training the local seminarians in scholastic philosophy and bringing to the whole country the so-called benefits of Western civilization. Many missionaries took it for granted that they should cooperate with the Western colonial powers. A friend of mine in the old days heard a classroom of Vietnamese children stand to attention and sing lustily, 'God bless France.' La gloire de la France!

In this context the Gospel was preached. And so the missionaries have been accused of destroying noble cultures, of depriving people of their native language, of being blind to the treasures of ancient civilizations, of alienating whole nations from their environment. Alas, alas, for the poor missionary. Once a glittering hero he has now hit the bottom rung of the totem pole.

But, again, let us not exaggerate. Let us be fair. Ricci and de Nobili loved their adopted culture. Their names are household words celebrated in song and in story. Nor are they alone. Thousands of others, like the great Protestant missionaries of the last century, were outstanding linguists and orientalists. They compiled dictionaries and grammars, studied the indigenous classics, mastered calligraphy, translated literary masterpieces. They are honoured today by the people they loved. Their names will never fade from the annals of history.

So much for the past. One cycle of missionary endeavour has come to an end. But every end is a beginning. A new, even more powerful, cycle is coming to birth. What will be its nature?

It seems to me that we must find a new and enlightened theology, purified from the old defects and based on Paul. That is to say we must find a new missionary theology based on love.

The days of the foreign missionary may be over but the words of Paul will never die. 'For necessity is laid on me. Woe to me if I do not preach the Gospel.' If only these words were engraved on the hearts of all Christians! Then, though we might not feel compelled, like Xavier, to travel far from home carrying the torch of faith, we would carry it to our own surroundings. Perhaps this is the way of the future. Already there is a vibrant movement for the evangelization of Europe and America. Undoubtedly Asians will come to help the West, as Westerners will go to help the East. There will be an interchange of personnel that will manifest the catholicity of Christian faith. But it will be different from the foreign missionary thrust that animated Xavier and his heroic followers when they went out 'to conquer new lands for Christ.' Indeed some religious congregations have stopped using the word mission (it somehow has a bad odour) and instead they speak of international apostolate.

But let me return to Paul. He did not, it seems, baptize many people. 'I am thankful that I baptized none of you except Crispus and Gaius', he writes to the Corinthians, 'lest anyone should say that you were baptized in my name. (I did baptize also the household of Stephanas. Beyond that, I do not know whether I baptized anyone else)' (1 Corinthians. 1:14). It was not that Paul considered baptism unimportant. Far from it. Some of his most wonderful rhetoric, as in *Romans*, is reserved for the beauty and value of baptism. Perhaps it was simply that baptising was not his charism. 'For Christ did not send me to baptize but to preach the Gospel . . . ' (1 Corinthians 1:17). He preached the Gospel and delegated the baptizing to others.

And many missionaries followed in his footsteps. Here in Japan, since the time of Meiji, Christian missionaries have built schools and hospitals and universities wherein they preached the Gospel without demanding baptism or affiliation to any Christian denomination. The result is that Gospel values have spread throughout the country. Everyone knows that, though statistically the number of baptized Japanese is abysmally small, the Christian influence is very great. Thousands, perhaps millions, of Japanese strive to live the Gospel without belonging to any church. Indeed a non-church movement, founded by the fervent Uchimura Kanzo, has attracted millions. I recall entering the room of one of my students and finding on the wall in big bold characters the words of Uchimura: 'I for Japan. Japan for the world. The world for Christ. And all for God.' The student was not, of course, baptized.

'Christ did not send me to baptize but to preach the Gospel. . .' There are many ways of preaching the Gospel. When you live the Gospel you preach the Gospel. When you love your neighbour you preach the Gospel. When you give a glass of water to a little one you preach the Gospel. When you struggle to liberate the oppressed you preach the Gospel. When you breathe your last you preach the Gospel. You preach the Gospel not only with your lips but with your whole body — even with your feet, as Paul says when he quotes the poetic words of Isaiah: 'How beautiful are the feet of those who preach good news!' (Romans 10:15) Throughout the modern world there is enormous scope for preaching the Gospel.

And is dialogue one way to live the Gospel? Is dialogue an authentic way to preach the Gospel? I think so.

But let me first say that dialogue is one of the great discoveries of the modern world. The conviction grows (and may it grow more and more!) that problems are not solved by altercation or violence or bloodshed but by talking and listening and working things out in an atmosphere of goodwill. So we have dialogue between nations, between husband and wife, between parents and children, between teacher and student, between lover and beloved, between rich and poor, between management and labour. In every section of society dialogue is the name of the game. And authentic dialogue is demanding! Yes, what else is new? Authentic dialogue is demanding. It asks us to be completely honest and frank, to respect human dignity, to forgive injuries, to listen and listen and listen, to be detached from our most cherished viewpoint, to compromise if necessary. Dialogue at its higher point asks for what is most painful to human nature: disinterested love. And what could be more in keeping with the Gospel?

The remarkable thing is that we have taken so long to discover this obvious aspect of the Gospel. It is just like non-violence. How long it took us to discover that waging war is not a good idea! How long it took us to discover that crusades and inquisitions and burning at the stake are not the way to preach the Gospel! And the person who finally enlightened us on this point was a Hindu: Mahatma Gandhi. And now I hope (I really do hope) we are discovering that to live the Gospel we must have dialogue both inside and outside the Church. This indeed was one of the principal messages of the Second Vatican Council.

But let me come to inter-religious dialogue which, while being most necessary, has its own peculiar challenges and problems.

Xavier and the early missionaries were not open to dialogue. As I have said, they believed that the unbaptized were on the path to destruction. Why listen to Satan? The task of the missionary, they believed, was to rescue souls from error and eternal fire. But happily Christianity has developed since those far-off days; and now we have a different theology.

The Second Vatican Council describes the Church as the people of God, embracing in some way not only Christians of all denominations but also Jews and Muslims, Buddhists and Hindus, people of goodwill everywhere and even well-intentioned atheists. The human race is one. Hand in hand we are journeying towards our common transcendent goal. John Paul put it well at Assisi where he invited religious leaders to pray for peace: '. . . We learn to walk together in peace and harmony, or we drift apart and ruin ourselves and others. We hope that this pilgrimage to Assisi has taught us anew to be aware of the common origin and common destiny of humanity. Let us see in it an anticipation of what God would like the developing history of humanity to be: a fraternal journey in which we accompany one another towards the transcendent goal which he sets for us.' Well said! We have come a long way since our 'outside the Church no salvation'.

Again, the Second Vatican Council spoke forthrightly about freedom of conscience in matters religious. Such is the sanctity, the inviolability of the human conscience that we must exert no pressure of any kind, nor force persons to change their religion. No more rice Christians. We must above all respect human dignity. We must respect human liberty. This, the Council claimed, is the authentic spirit of the Gospel.

Again, we now appreciate the richness of diverse cultures through the world; and we can distinguish between religion and culture. We know (and now it seems so obvious) that to preach the Gospel is not to preach the Western culture in which it developed for many centuries. Christians everywhere now love the local culture. They are bending their backs to the gigantic task of inculturation.

And this new context enables us to preach the Gospel sincerely through dialogue.

In dialogue we preach the Gospel in its entirety. Anything else would be unfair to the people we address. Just as we want to hear the whole *dharma*, so they want to hear the whole Gospel. The first things are sincerity, honesty, love of truth. We must be true to ourselves, as we ask others to be true to themselves. 'For necessity is laid on me, woe to me if I do not preach the Gospel.'

Secondly we must listen. We must listen, believing that the Spirit may speak powerfully to us through Buddhists, Hindus, Muslims, Jews. This does not mean we accept every word they say, as they need not accept every word we say. But we do listen.

And what a challenge this is! For Buddhism is a beautiful religion, an attractive religion, a fascinating religion. It offers deep religious experience, profound enlightenment and liberation from suffering. To gaze at a statue of the Buddha is to be drawn into the silent oneness of contemplation. Encountering Buddhism, we Christians may feel threatened and unsure; we may feel tempted to question our Christian commitment. Or we may take the tack of down-grading Buddhism, protesting triumphantly that its teaching is already implicitly contained in our own tradition. 'Why listen to Buddhism? It's all in Augustine.' How often we hear such nonsense!

But if we persevere in our journey through the storms of dialogue we come to deep inner peace in the appreciation of what is essential in our own faith and what we can profitably learn from Buddhism. We strengthen our commitment to Jesus; we see that one who loves the Gospel loves all religions and cultures.

Woe to me if I do not preach the Gospel! In dialogue we preach the entire Gospel because we love the Gospel and want to share its treasures with people we love. We put no pressure on anyone to accept it. No beguiling promises. No stern threats. No charming enticements. No malicious bribes. No backstairs politics. Paul offered nothing except Christ crucified. 'For I decided to know nothing among you except Jesus Christ and Him crucified' (1 Corinthians 2:2). And so it is entirely up to those who hear our word. They accept what they want; they leave what they don't want. We never break into the inner sanctum of conscience where the human person is alone with God.

And this demands detachment. It demands that detachment from the fruit of our labour that is stressed in the *Bhagavad Gita* and was so dear to the heart of Mahatma Gandhi. It demands purity of intention. We preach the Gospel because we preach the Gospel. The East loves the perfection of action — the purity of one who does things because he does them, not from fear of punishment or hope of reward.

And this is disinterested love. In our missionary endeavour we have been greatly influenced by a spirituality of conquest — of conquering lands for Christ. Perhaps this spirituality arose in medieval Europe with the crusades and the wars against the Moors. But now we must remember that the Church, like its founder, comes to serve and not to be served. The aim of the Church is not to conquer the world but to serve the world. So let us serve the world, putting less emphasis on statistics and numbers of baptisms. Let us aim at the disinterested love that looks for no reward.

Having said all this I am aware that a major problem remains.

The truth is that Asia will accept the Gospel with open arms — and has done so. The problem is baptism; the problem is conversion to the Christian community. I myself know parents who are anxious to have their children learn the Gospel, but are adamant that their children will not be baptized. And this has been a problem all over Asia. People feel that in changing their religious commitment they are deserting their friends, betraying their ancestors, abandoning their history. And in spite of all our efforts at inculteration, this problem remains.

Yet if we preach the Gospel in its entirety, we must preach baptism — conversion to Jesus and the Christian community. Not, I say it again, that we force anyone or utter stern threats. But the Gospel itself demands this. Remember that Paul cried out to Agrippa: 'I would to God that not only you but all who hear me this day might become such as I am — except for these chains' (Acts 26:29). And in making this conversion Paul 'suffered the loss of all things' as did many, many converts like John Henry Newman. 'Lead, kindly light . . .'

And if in the inner sanctum of conscience people ask for baptism, we welcome them into the Christian community. And we ask people in Asia to recognize freedom of conscience in this most sacred area of religion. We know that this is painful for everyone. It is the pain of human life lived with authenticity.

But there is one important corollary. We, too, must recognize the conscience of those who would leave the Gospel for Buddhism or Islam. This is very painful for us. It is particularly painful because our whole tradition from the earliest times recoils from what we called *apostasy*; and we pray: 'Put us not to the test.' But if we are true to the Gospel we recognize the sanctity of the human conscience even when we are baffled by its mystery.

I have talked longer than I intended. I only hope it was under the guidance of the Spirit.

I was glad to hear that you and Frank are meditating together. Yes, I agree that a mysticism of interpersonal relations is possible and, indeed, that it is the way of the future. I smiled at your comment about the dark night of marriage. Ha! Ha! I can well imagine it. But remember that the darkest night comes just before the dawn of enlightenment. So keep going!

I leave for Manila next week on the first leg of my sabbatical. Frank has my address and I look forward to hearing from both of you.

Greetings again to both of you and to the children. You are always in my prayers.

Bill J——— S.J.

Dear Maria,

Your letter, redirected from Tokyo, caught up with me here in the Philippines. It was good to hear from you and to know that all is going well. I am enjoying Manila. As you know, I spent a few years here at the beginning of the 1980s during the Marcos regime. And I came to love the Philippinos. For all the poverty, they are a happy people, always smiling and enjoying the joke. And they are so musical — everyone seems to play the guitar and sing. Someone once remarked to me that the vocation of the Philippinos is to carry music and faith to the world. And that makes sense. There is a lot of faith here and I have been impressed by the huge congregations lustily singing the Our Father in Tagalog and celebrating the Eucharist with evident fervour. For one interested in religious experience — even in things like shamanism — this country is a treasure-house. Quite honestly I don't know what to make of the faith-healing and the weird psychic surgery and people getting themselves crucified and what not. It baffles me; and I can only say with Hamlet: 'There are more things in heaven and earth, Horatio, than are dreamt of in your philosophy.'

But to come to your letter. You ask if mysticism is possible for a married woman. You say that you feel called to deep prayer but do not quite see your path, and you ask what I think.

Your question is both simple and complicated. Of course it is possible for a married person to attain to the very pinnacle of mysticism. And knowing you as I do, your deep faith, your sense of God's presence, your love for your family, your concern for the poor, I feel quite sure that you are called. You have the further advantage that David is a deeply prayerful person. It matters not that his spiritual path is a bit different from yours. Walk together. Two mystics — ha! ha! So, Maria, surrender to God and go on your way with confidence and joy.

Yet I do see the difficulties. The first is that most of the literature on mysticism has been written by celibates for celibates — as though

27

mysticism was the preserve of monks and nuns. Alas, the Catholic tradition is not free from elitism. *The Cloud of Unknowing*, for example, written in fourteenth-century England, distinguishes between those called to salvation and those called to perfection. Those called to salvation are the masses of the people, the laity — and for these the author will write no mystical treatise. Those called to perfection are the monks and nuns (and perhaps priests and bishops are thrown in) and for them mysticism is a real possibility. And this way of thinking held the field until the Second Vatican Council.

It is true, of course, that St Francis de Sales wrote for married people in the seventeenth century, and his *Devout Life* is a classic which will help you a lot. It is also true that some mystical theologians of the nineteenth and early twentieth centuries spoke about the universal call to contemplation or mysticism. But these good men were celibates, thinking about the celibate path. They were not catering for people like you and David.

The distinction between those called to salvation and those called to perfection was hit on the head by the Second Vatican Council (1962-5), which declared that every Christian is called to perfection. By reason of baptism, said the Council, every Christian is called to holiness and at times even to martyrdom; for all are called to love God with their whole heart and soul and mind and strength. The Council also spoke enthusiastically about holiness in the family, hinting at a mysticism of interpersonal relations and saying that in marriage 'authentic human love is caught up into divine love.'

The latter phrase intrigues me, and I ask myself what it means. I suppose it means that human love is progressively divinized until the spouses love one another and their children with the love of God Himself. Mysticism with a vengeance! And I ask myself by what process authentic human love is caught up into divine love. Is it by prayer in common? Or is it by uncompromising fidelity to another person? Really I must confess that I am not competent to advise you in this area (for, as you know, I am an incorrigible celibate) and you and David, together with thousands of modern people are pioneers in the search for mysticism in family life and for a mysticism of sexuality.

One thing is clear. You will experience God as a wife and mother, just as David will experience God as a husband and father — and you both have your work. Quite a challenge! You are called to experience God in all things: in household chores, in the family, on the bus, at your office. Gradually, O so gradually, you will come to feel the presence of God in all the events of life in accordance with that little book by a Franciscan Brother *The Practice of the Presence of God.* I recommend it heartily.

Since in the mystical life one is purified by both action and suffering, remember that a great purification will take place through the struggles of married life. Again I am not qualified to speak about this; but the growing divorce rate, the frequency of infidelity, the talk of marriage as a disaster area, the plethora of books on making marriage work, all highlight the intense suffering that necessarily accompanies marriage. And then the education of children in our drug-infested, alcohol-drenched society, to say nothing of the misunderstandings and disappointments in interpersonal relationships — all this suffering can constitute a dark night that is no less purifying than St John of the Cross's dark night of the soul. And it leads to an intimacy and a union and a spiritual marriage that is consummated beyond the grave. Again, you and David are in a better position to explore this than am I.

I advise you together, or with other married couples who have similar aspirations, to read the Council's section on marriage in 'The Church in the Modern World'. You will find there a basis for mysticism in married life.

The fact is that we are in a new age; and it is the age of the laity. Everyone knows that religious life is in decline because (and this is just my opinion) religious orders and congregations have lost their mysticism. At the same time we find extraordinarily fervent lay people everywhere. Here in the Philippines the laity have courageously taken on responsibility both in the sacramental life and in the struggle for justice. Then think of China! When history is written we will hear of extraordinary heroism among thousands of Chinese men and women; we will hear of their cruel imprisonment, their constancy under torture, their glorious martyrdom. Never again will we be able to distinguish between a laity called to salvation and religious called to perfection. And you yourselves know about the zeal and devotion of thousands (shall

I say millions?) of US Christians who are totally devoted to Jesus Christ and to the struggle for a more just society.

Interestingly enough, Buddhism also has come into its age of the laity. Primitive Buddhism, particularly Theravada Buddhism, was deeply monastic; but now in Japan we see the rise of new Buddhist sects with millions of adherents, all of whom are lay people. No monks! No clergy! No clericalism! And in Zen, which was originally monastic, some of the leading masters are laymen, married men who have brought up a family, retired from business and now devote themselves to the Buddha, the *dharma*, the *sangha*. Will a similar phenomenon appear within the Christian Church? Admittedly not many women are in roles of leadership in Japan but the women's hour will come soon, very soon.

What I am trying to say is that the movement towards lay leadership and initiative is undoubtedly the work of the Spirit in the whole world.

But to get to your main point. Can I recommend something practical? You say that mysticism takes time, time, time. You say that mystics retire for years to a cave in the mountains or a hut in the desert — and that is not your cup of tea. What with a house to clean, business letters to type, children to put to bed, dinners to cook, time is a luxury seldom found. I understand. My own mother used to quote Virginia Woolf who spoke of women as 'the interrupted sex'. Interruption all day.

Perhaps this difficulty is not unsurmountable. I said that most books on mysticism were written for celibate religious. There is, however, one resounding exception: the New Testament. Matthew, Mark, Luke and John wrote for you and David. And then St Paul. Who was he addressing when he said: 'But we impart a secret and hidden wisdom of God, which God decreed before the ages for our glorification' (1 Corinthians 2:7). This secret and hidden wisdom is mysticism — for the word mystical means secret or hidden. And Paul was talking to ordinary, hard-boiled Corinthians. I advise you to read the New Testament with David. If you try to *live* the Gospel you'll find it extremely radical and demanding. You will find there the 'all and nothing': you leave all you possess and have nothing in order to find all.

And that brings me to the Carmelite mystics: John and Teresa.

They wrote for members of their own order: their teaching is geared to men and women consecrated by the three vows. However, there is a third order of Carmel for lay people — the so-called tertiaries. They are flourishing here in the Philippines and in the US. With striking success they are attempting to adapt Carmelite mysticism to the active life of lay people. Carmelite priests and sisters have told me that it is precisely the tertiaries who will carry the spirit of Teresa and John into the next century.

Then there is St Ignatius, our Jesuit founder. His teaching is eminently suited to the laity; for he believed in the value of short prayer. He said (and this was drilled into us in the noviceship) that the mortified person would achieve more in fifteen minutes than the unmortified in several hours. He raised Cain when some of his disciples proposed spending seven years in solitude before embarking on an apostolic career. His was a mysticism of seeing God in all things, of experiencing God in the hurly-burly of life. He loved the mighty cities and I suppose he would have loved the noisy household. He had an insight that Zen people would undoubtedly support; namely, that what matters is not long time spent in prayer but loss of the ego. And one loses the ego by following Jesus, poor, despised and humiliated. It has been said that Ignatius preferred ascetics to mystics. I prefer to say that he liked a healthy mysticism built on a healthy asceticism.

And so I recommend the Spiritual Exercises. If possible, do them with David. Today you don't need to enclose yourself in a retreat house; you can do 'the exercises in daily life' while continuing your ordinary work.

Choose a good director. Light has been thrown on the Exercises by renewed interest in the autobiography of St Ignatius. This little book, a gem of mystical literature, was neglected for centuries — perhaps because of current fears of illuminism and false mysticism. Now it comes to a central position in Jesuit spirituality, revealing an Ignatius who was strongly, even embarrassingly, mystical. Read in the light of this autobiography the Exercises become a school of contemplative prayer, contemplative prayer that vibrates through a life of intense activity. Whereas the Exercises were formerly given in a plodding, natural way, they can now be a school of mysticism.

Yet another phenomenon worth investigating is the Oriental meditation movement now popular in the Western world. You may have heard of the Benedictine monk John Main, who taught mantra meditation in Britain and Canada. The mantra he recommended was 'Maranatha' — Come, Lord Jesus'; and his way is profoundly Christian, filled with the presence of Jesus. Again, there is centring prayer, practised widely in the US. In this whole matter the best advice I can give is to be open to the Spirit who will guide you to the prayer that suits you.

Please let me know how things are going.

I'll be here in the Philippines for a couple of weeks, during which time I'll make a brief visit to Mindanao in the South. I have many friends there and I look forward to meeting them. As you must know, Mindanao is the home of a flourishing Islamic culture which, alas, has been at war with the predominantly Christian culture in the rest of the Philippines. One of the top priorities of the Philippino Church and, indeed, of the Philippino Government is to promote good relations between Christians and Muslims. That's a challenge. We all want peace; but we don't always want the things that lead to peace!

Greetings to David and the children. May God bless you all!

Bill J——— S.J.

Manila
30 April 1989

Dear Ayako,

I write this letter in the sweltering heat of Manila. What a change
from Tokyo! The smog and the air pollution and the noise in Cubao
are out of this world — positively frightening. One lives perpetually
bathed in perspiration and surrounded by hooting and hullabaloo.
And then the heart-rending sight of young women carrying their
babies in the middle of the road, groping through the traffic, begging
for alms! People have told me these women are professional beggars.
But that makes the whole scene no less painful.

   Apologies for such a lugubrious beginning. What I want to say
is that it was very kind of you to come to Narita to see me off. I
appreciate that a lot. And I have been thinking about our
conversation at the airport. We asked who were the great mystics
of our time and whether people like Merton and C.S. Lewis and
Mother Teresa could be called mystics or whether that word should
be preserved for extraordinary personalities like Padre Pio and
Abhishiktananda and Ramana Maharshi. And then we talked about
the visionaries in Medugorje.

   Now it seems to me that probably we will never know the great
mystics of our day. Probably they are simple, unknown people who
never heard the word mystic and are highly favoured by God. St
Therese of Lisieux became known because she wrote her
autobiography; but there must be thousands or millions of Therese's
in all religions who never write a line, and whose profound
relationship with God will only be known at the eschaton when the
last will be first and the first last.

   Religious life, of course, should be a school of contemplation;
and I believe there are plenty of contemplatives among those who
have taken the three vows. St John of the Cross keeps saying that
many people arrive at a good but superficial level of contemplation.
They reach the prayer of quiet — but very few plumb the depths
or go the whole hog. And I think that is true today. I wonder why.
It may simply be that they are not called. But one reason is that

33

we don't have directors. Here we can learn from Buddhism where the art of direction is highly developed or from Hinduism which has a special place for the guru. As for the visionaries of Medugorje — that's different kettle of fish. I plan to visit Medugorje while in Europe and I'll let you know how I feel about it.

But you may be wondering how things have gone with me here. Well, after a couple of days in Manila I flew down to Mindanao in the South. This is the Islamic part of the Philippines; and in Zamboanga I found a flourishing dialogue between Muslims and Christians.

It all began some years ago, during the Marcos regime, when a fervent young Muslim girl, fleeing from the military, took refuge in a Carmelite monastery. A deep friendship quickly developed between this girl and one of the sisters, and that was the beginning of a dialogue that has grown and grown. What is interesting about this dialogue is that it is based primarily on prayer and contemplation. I don't need to tell you that Muslims have a profound sense of prayer, as Charles de Foucauld and Carlo Carretto discovered in the African desert. And I myself have been impressed by the sight of Muslims praying publicly in the streets of Cairo. Anyhow, in Zamboanga a group of Christians are now in ongoing dialogue with Muslims, and things are beginning to happen. They have a monthly publication called *Silsilah*, and on the cover of my copy I see: 'Islamo-Christian Silsilah (chain) is a dialogue movement promoting deeper understanding and better relations between Muslims and Christians with particular emphasis on the spiritual dimensions of dialogue.' While this dialogue is based on prayer, it is by no means indifferent to justice and injustice — nor to the extremely distressful economic and political situation of this country. It concentrates on promoting peace and harmony.

I am fascinated by the way this dialogue began; that is, through deep friendship between a Muslim and a Christian. Surely this is the crown of authentic dialogue: friendship. And friendship, the Gospel tells us, demands equality and is proved by willingness to lay down one's life for the person one loves. When men and women of the world religions form such friendships, dialogue will really be meaningful. And will that day come? I know that in Northern Ireland there are deep friendships between Christians of different denominations and our hope for the future lies in that. At the risk of sounding facetious (and you may laugh if you like) I might say that the all-time dialogue was between Romeo and Juliet. It was over the lovers' dead bodies that the houses of Capulet and Montague were finally reconciled.

But the Islamo-Christian dialogue in Mindanao interests me from another standpoint.

With the collapse of communism it becomes increasingly clear that the great political and religious force of the future will be Islam. And Islam will be powerful not only in the great crescent that runs from North Africa to Indonesia and Mindanao but also in Europe. Already mosques are burgeoning in London and Paris and other European cities as the followers of the Prophet increase in numbers. What does the future hold? Will it be possible for Muslims and Christians to enter into dialogue after the pattern of the group in Zamboanga?

We all sincerely hope so. But, of course, there will be difficulties. Already we have seen the turmoil aroused by *The Satanic Verses*. We have seen the uproar in France and Britain when Muslim girls refused to remove their headscarfs (hidjab) in the classroom. I myself think the Muslim headscarf is very beautiful and I wouldn't dream of asking anyone to take it off. But that is by the way. We hear of discrimination against the Turkish *gastarbeiters* in Germany. This together with European fear of what is happening in the Middle East makes Muslim-Christian dialogue a challenging proposition.

Moreover, in the meeting of Muslims and Christians we cannot forget history. There has been a long, long war between Islam and Christendom; and thinking people are asking if it could all begin again — if the peaceful centuries since the Renaissance were no more than a long truce, if the rumblings in Britain and France and Germany indicate that Europe is sitting on a smouldering volcano.

For the sad fact is that a deep fear of Islam lurks ominously in the unconscious of Europe. It goes right back to the collapse of the Roman Empire when Europe fell into the so-called Dark Ages while a flourishing Islamic culture rose throughout the Middle East and North Africa. Islam became a mighty power that threatened to overwhelm a poor little Europe emerging from barbarism and savagery. When I was a small boy at school in Liverpool, I learned how in AD 732 Charles Martel, leader of the Franks, gloriously defeated the Moors at the Battle of Tours, thus saving Europe from Islam. For this he was honoured with the title of defender of Christendom. We had a holiday from school (great fun that was) to watch a movie in which Richard the Lionheart led his men gallantly into battle against Saladdin. What a hero was Richard! And how tragically noble were the Crusaders! This was the time when G.K. Chesterton was composing his stirring ballad about Don John of Austria and the victory of Lepanto, while his fighting friend Hilaire Belloc was ominously warning the West of the peril of another Islamic invasion. I was in England. But no doubt children in Spain and Portugal were learning about the expulsion of the Moors from the Iberian peninsula in 1492; and German children learned the sad story of how Constantinople fell to the Turks in 1453. All in all, even in the twentieth century Europe was conscious of its very old war with a violent Islam symbolized by the fearful scimitar and the crescent.

And Europe did not fight with the sword alone. After the Crusaders a rabid propaganda war was waged against Islam. Staunch Christian writers thought they could do no greater service to God than by attacking Islam as an evil empire, the enemy of civilization. Medieval biographies vilified the Prophet in language that makes Salman Rushdie sound like an innocent lamb. Like many Christians who have travelled in the Middle East, the thirteenth-century Dominican, Ricoldo da Monte Cruce, was impressed by the prayerful spirit of the Muslims; but he remained deeply prejudiced. His *Disputation Against the Saracens and the Koran* repeats the old vicious propaganda. And his book was a standard text in Europe until the end of the seventeenth century.

We now know how unfair all this was. It was inspired, no doubt, by fear of the immense religious power of Muhammad and his followers. In the beginning Islam was not violent and was able to live peacefully with other religions. The Koran told them to respect Jews and Christians. Their prayer to Allah was powerful and profound. Their philosophy was second to none. But, as I have said, it was the fear of a threatening religion that found its way into the European consciousness and lurks dangerously there in our very day.

Needless to say there were faults on both sides, as there were crusades on both sides. And a propaganda war was waged also by Muslims. Moreover, some Christians loved and respected Islam. Eminent among these is St Francis of Assisi. Then there is the thirteenth-century Spanish poet and mystic, Raymond Lull. Brought up among the Moors in Majorca he learned Arabic and wrote in that language. One of his works is a conversation between a Muslim, a Christian and a Jew searching for common ground. Then there was Aquinas. No doubt his approach to Islam was polemical (after all, he was a man of his time) but it was profoundly respectful. He probably realized that Arabic philosophy was superior to anything that had developed in Europe — it had preserved the works of Aristotle and given birth to thinkers of the stature of Averroes and Avicenna. Against them he wrote his *Summa contra Gentiles*; but he was prepared to learn from them. And the whole scholastic movement that followed Aquinas had to acknowledge its debt to Arabic thinkers.

Having said this, however, it remains true that the prevailing climate in Europe was deeply prejudiced against Islam. And that European prejudice spilled over into the Philippines where Spanish missionaries went to preach the Gospel. As Christians did a service to God by driving the Muslims out of Spain, so Christians did a service to God by driving Muslims out of Luzon and the Northern Islands down to Mindanao. But whereas there was a long truce in Europe, the war in the Philippines never ceased—until now in the 1990s a tiny group of Muslims and a tiny group of Christians are trying to beat their swords into ploughshares and search for reconciliation. Will Europeans be able to follow their example?

As we look at today's world we see a different Europe. The old Christendom has gone the way of all flesh, and in its place stands a post-Christian, secularized continent in which committed Christians are a minority. And the Christian community has been revolutionized in its thinking by a Second Vatican Council (1962-5) which asked us to follow the Gospel in banishing war from the face of the earth and loving all men and women as well as all religions and all cultures. In this atmosphere it should be possible for Christians to stretch out a hand of friendship to Muslims and to pray for profound reconciliation.

But we must take the Council seriously.

First, the Council said that there can be no ecumenism worthy of the name without conversion of heart. It was speaking, of course, about ecumenism within Christianity, but the same principles apply to our relationship with other religions. The Council quoted Paul: 'I, therefore, the prisoner in the Lord, exhort you to walk in a manner worthy of the calling with which you were called, with all humility and meekness, with patience, bearing with one another in love, careful to preserve the unity of the Spirit in the bond of peace' (Ephesians 4: 1-3). It then goes on to ask forgiveness for our sins: 'Thus, in humble prayer, we beg pardon of God and of our separated brethren, just as we forgive those who trespass against us.'

And what a conversion of heart is needed in our relationship with Islam! A conversion of heart that will penetrate to the deepest levels of the unconscious mind, eliminating or healing our fear and anger and prejudice, thus making way for love. And will the day come when we can ask Islamic forgiveness for all that happened in the past? Such a conversion can only come about by God's grace which is given through prayer and fasting.

Again, the Council emphasized that we must come to understand the outlook of our separated brethren. 'Study is absolutely required for this, and should be pursued with fidelity to truth and in a spirit of good will.' And elsewhere the Council said that we should be fair.

Let me here pause to say that Christian theologians have as yet made mighty little effort to understand Buddhism, Hinduism and Islam or to study these religions with good will and fidelity to the truth. It is sad to hear distinguished theologians and high-ranking ecclesiastics make solemn pronouncements about Buddhist meditation without knowing the most elementary facts. And will they now go on to make profound statements about Islam based on what they have read in the *Daily Express*? 'Study is absolutely necessary,' said the Council, 'and should be pursued with fidelity to truth.' So let us be fair. Let us play the game.

If we study Islam with good will and fidelity to the truth we will find treasures of spiritual insight. The Council spoke of Islam's adoration of one God, living and enduring, merciful and all-powerful, Maker of heaven and earth and Speaker to men and women. It spoke of the Muslims' reverence for Abraham — and for Jesus and Mary. It spoke of their belief in an after life, of their high morality, of their prayer, alms giving and fasting. Just as we Christians rightly feel distressed when our adversaries judge Christianity not by the Gospel but by some of the deviations and skulduggery and real evils of the medieval Church, so Muslims rightly feel indignant if we fasten on their defects and deviations while neglecting the Koran and the authentic Islamic tradition. Again, let us be fair.

And if Muslims and Christians can unite (while respecting the obvious differences in faith) what a contribution we can make to the new Europe!

For the plain truth is that the decline of Europe has been brought about by atheism. I am reminded of *Romans* where Paul traces the collapse of Rome to the forgetfulness of God. 'For although they knew God they did not honour Him as God or give thanks to Him, but they became futile in their thinking and their senseless minds were darkened' (Romans 1: 21). And from this rejection of God flowed all the other evils. And can we not say the same of large sections of Europe which want neither God nor Allah nor Jesus nor the Prophet?

If only the day would come when Muslims and Jews and Christians would pray side by side to the one God whom we all worship. What a contribution that would make to Europe and to world peace!

A while ago I saw a picture in *The Times* of Muslims praying in the streets of London. What a shock to the Brits! And to the Irish and the French and the Germans. We have all forgotten about prayer in the market-place.

And the answer to atheism is not academic controversy but prayer. Thanks to our Muslim brethren the time may again come when prayer is respectable and when theology is discussed in the leading newspapers. It may be that the gross materialism that has characterized our century is coming to an end. If so, all the religions will have their role to play in building a new world. Only let us love one another. Let us not fight.

Well, I have written more than I intended. I hope your own writing is going well. I look forward to seeing some of your articles. If you are interested in writing something about this dialogue in the

Philippines I can send you a few copies of *Silsilah*.

Next week I leave for sunny California. I'll stop off at Honolulu and then on to San Francisco. I'm never happier than when climbing onto a jet!

God bless you, and keep smiling.

Bill J————— S. J.

Santa Clara University
California
15 May 1989

Dear Jack,

Your letter was waiting for me when I arrived. The flight from Manila was long and tiring; but at last I'm over the jet lag and have settled in sunny California. The campus here is superb. The gardens are aglow with beauty — with geraniums red and delphiniums blue besides all kinds of white and yellow flowers whose names I do not know. And, then there are two swimming-pools. The university has given me a fellowship, which leaves me time for reading and writing and swimming. Add to this the good company (good crack we say in Ireland) in the community; and what could be better?

I'm preparing a book on mystical theology. As you know, I am convinced that one of the tragedies of Western Christianity is that we have lost our mysticism. Of course there are some mystics around; but mysticism does not play a central role in our religious outlook; and in our seminaries mystical theology is of minor importance. But as I look to the future, particularly to the dialogue with Buddhism, Hinduism and Islam, I feel sure that mystical theology will occupy the centre of the picture. Besides, I foresee a great revival of religion in Russia. And when the West comes face to face with a profound Russian spirituality purified by decades of suffering — then our speculative theologians will look like pygmies as the giants of Russian mysticism rise to the heavens.

I already wrote a book on mystical theology — it was my doctoral thesis — entitled *The Mysticism of 'The Cloud of Unknowing'*. This treats of mysticism against a background of scholastic philosophy and theology. In the next book I'd like to continue with the apophatic tradition; but instead of scholasticism I'll be open to Buddhist philosophy and to psychologists like Jung. That's the challenge!

And a mystical theology would tackle the very problem you bring up in your letter: interpersonal relationships. You, a Catholic priest

41

committed to celibacy, are searching for friendship and deep intimacy with both men and women. And you say you need guidance.

In all this you are a truly modern person. Everywhere in today's world one finds a great search, sometimes an anguished search, for human love and intimacy. Some prophets of philosophy even predict that as the last millennium was devoted to the theoretical exploration of cognition, the next millennium will be devoted to the theoretical exploration of love. I certainly hope so. And I would add (and this is where the mystics come in) that we will not understand human love until we probe deeply into the mystery of divine love. For the two are inextricably intertwined.

And men and women consecrated to God know full well that their vow of chastity does not mean the sacrifice of human love and friendship and intimacy. How could it possibly mean that? Didn't the Council speak of the companionship of man and woman as 'the primary form of interpersonal communication'?

So you walk the path of love and intimacy. But do not be too idyllic about it. For what suffering compares with the suffering of love? Think of Hosea! Think of the tragic Madame Butterfly and her sad, sad song. And hasn't that song been sung by thousands upon thousands? 'If by chance you see him I love most,' cries St John of the Cross, 'tell him that I sicken, suffer and die.' And Paul's anguished love for his own people! 'I have great sorrow and unceasing anguish in my heart. For I could wish that I myself were accursed and cut off from Christ for the sake of my brethren, my kinsmen by race' (Romans 9:2). Human love, divine love, any kind of love can be an open wound, albeit a joyful wound, that only the beloved can heal.

Read the Scriptures and you will find that a central theme is marriage. And there are two marriages. The principal one is the covenant, which is the marriage between Yaweh and the people of Israel. For Yaweh is the bridegroom and the people are the bride while human life is one great love affair. 'Let me sing for my beloved a love song concerning his vineyard . . .' (Isaiah 5:1). And later, in the New Testament, Jesus is the bridegroom while the Christian community is his bride. And later still, in the mystical tradition, Jesus is the bridegroom, while the individual

42

human person, whether masculine or feminine, is his bride. And underlying this is the basic message that we are all created for union with Jesus in a marriage that will be consummated in the eschaton.

But there is also human marriage between man and woman; and there is human friendship between people of the same sex or of opposite sexes. And these relationships are symbols or signs of the covenant, pointing to a reality that will not pass. 'The children of this age marry and are given in marriage; but those who are accounted worthy to attain to that age and to the resurrection from the dead neither marry nor are given in marriage, for they cannot die any more, because they are equal to angels and are children of God, being children of the resurrection' (Luke 20:36). In the resurrection, then, is consummated the real marriage for which human beings were created.

Influenced by Freudian psychology we tend to reverse the order of divine providence, saying that human sexual intercourse is the reality and that marriage with God is some dream. Hence the literature about St Teresa of Avila and other mystics, indicating that their spiritual marriage was a sublimation of their frustrated sexual drives. Yet the traditional Christian teaching still stands: authentic celibates choose the reality towards which sexual intercourse points and of which sexual intercourse is a sacramental symbol. To sacrifice the symbol for the eschalological reality is legitimate and reasonable.

Paul speaks of the love of Jesus for the community as the model, the basic reality towards which human love points:

'Husbands, love your wives, as Christ loved the church and gave himself up for her' (Ephesians 5:25). But when he has struggled through a few tortured sentences of explanation he adds: 'This is a great mystery. . . .' How true! All this is mysteriously built on faith and I would make no attempt to demonstrate it rationally to one who does not believe.

Enough of mystery. Let me come to practicalities.

Human love and human intimacy are a reflection of the divine intimacy that fills the scriptures. In the Christian tradition we find plenty of saints and mystics speaking about intimacy with God, intimacy with Jesus, intimate friendship with the Lord. And this divine intimacy spilled over into their relationships with Peter and Jane and Joseph. They loved their friends with the same love with which they loved Jesus. If married, they loved their families with that love too.

Yes, as we grow in intimacy with God and with his only Son in prayer, we grow in intimacy with other men and women. That is why human intimacy has an important place in a modern mystical theology. Prayer, and particularly contemplative prayer, liberates us from the craving and clinging and projection and anguish that mar deep intimacy. Prayer opens up new levels of consciousness that are ordinarily dormant. It gives birth to the living flame of love which goes out not only to God our Father but to all men and women and to the very environment in which we live. Through prayer human love becomes a participation in that divine love by which Jesus loved his disciples and loves us. So persevere in prayer, open your heart to the deepest contemplation, remembering that if you are loving and contemplative in your prayer you will be loving and contemplative in your human relationships.

It is true that modern people are baffled by the mention of celibate love and celibate intimacy, yet this is the most common of all loves. Parents who love their children, children who love their parents, brothers and sisters who love one another, friends who drink beer and coffee together — isn't their love celibate? And do they not have moments of the most profound intimacy?

And this love shines through every page of the Gospel. It is love for the other as she is in herself. It is the love of Peter, who said: 'Lord, you know that I love you.' It is the love of the good Samaritan who took tenderly into his arms the wounded Jew who lay by the roadside. It is the love of the woman who wet the feet of Jesus with her tears, and wiped them with the hair of her head, and kissed his feet, and anointed them with ointment. It is the love of Martha and Mary. It is the love of one who lays down his life for his friend. And all points to the love of the Heavenly Father who makes the rain fall on the just and the unjust and gives sunshine to everyone.

Jesus distinguishes between love for the servant and love for the friend. And this is important for one who aspires to intimacy. The servant does not know what his master is doing, thinking and saying. 'But I have called you friends, for all that I have heard from my

Father I have made known to you' (John 15:15). In friendship love is mutual: I love and am loved. And it culminates in a total self-revelation: 'All that I have heard from my Father . . .'. What remarkable luminosity of one person to another! And this self-revelation has one extraordinary consequence: it leads to mutual indwelling.

At the beginning of the fourth gospel the two disciples ask Jesus: 'Rabbi (which means Teacher) where are you staying?' (John 1:38) It is as though they wanted to make their home in him. And Jesus replied: 'Come and see', as he was to say in another gospel 'Come to me, all you who labour and are heavy laden, and I will give you rest' (Matthew 11:28). And the last discourse of the fourth gospel is filled with the notion of indwelling. The disciples dwell in Jesus as the branch dwells in the vine. 'Abide in me, and I in you . . . abide in my love.' And: 'In that day you will know that I am in my Father, and you in me, and I in you.'

No doubt the author of the fourth gospel had his gaze fixed on The Risen Jesus and on the Eucharist; for it is here that indwelling reaches its highest point. But no doubt he also believed that there was a deep relationship of indwelling between the historical Jesus and the disciples with whom he broke bread. In other words, some measure of indwelling, however imperfect, is possible in this valley of tears.

And so to your question: Is this mutual indwelling possible in human friendship so that one friend can say to another: 'As the Father has loved me I have loved you; dwell in my love'? Is it possible even when these friends live on opposite sides of the globe?

I believe it is possible — but only after long and painful purification. For the sad fact is that human nature, wounded and torn by sickness and sin, can only come to authentic love by passing through torment and fire.

For human love can be addictive — as addictive as alcohol or tobacco or drugs — and the road from addiction to freedom is never easy. Even when authentic, human love can be marred by jealousy, fear, anger, anxiety, possessiveness, love-hate and a host of little foxes that render indwelling quite impossible. Add to this the mysterious fear of intimacy, the fear of opening the door to another person. Such is the human condition. And, needless to say,

45

contemplatives suffer this like anyone else. Think of Thomas Merton!

In the old ascetical tradition contemplatives were told to break addictive relationships instantly, saying to the other: 'Henceforth you go your way and I go mine.' We were even encouraged to surround ourselves with a wall of reserve, to feel nothing, to protect ourselves from the seductive other. What a strange misunderstanding of the Gospel! 'Get thee to a nunnery, go; farewell . . . To a nunnery, go, and quickly, too. Farewell.' Poor Hamlet — and poor Ophelia! Were nunneries and monasteries havens of refuge, escapes from the cruel demands of human love? I hope not.

Today we are more enlightened. While we see that addictive relationships must sometimes be quickly terminated, we also see that they can be purified in such ways that they become authentic and loving, leading to God and the upbuilding of the universe. And I believe that Jungian psychology throws some light on this painful process of purification.

I am greatly taken by Jung's theory of animus and anima — which owes much to the Chinese yin and yang. Every man has a feminine dimension called anima — for no man is totally masculine; and every woman has a masculine dimension called animus — for no woman is totally feminine. In some ideal world (perhaps it was that way in the Garden of Eden) we would be whole, integrated, innocent; but alas we are no longer in the state of original justice. Fallen humans, we are inwardly divided; we lack integrity or wholeness; we reject parts of ourselves; and in particular we reject our contrasexual dimension. Or we let our animus or anima float around to be projected on a person of the opposite sex. When this happens, our relationship becomes addictive, compulsive, unfree. Imagining that we love the other, we love ourselves in the other. We are drugged.

So the great challenge is to withdraw the contrasexual projection — to integrate it, to become a whole person, to become one's true self. In other words the great challenge is to enact the interior marriage between the animus and the anima. And when the interior marriage is consummated one is able to love the other as she is in herself, with freedom and joy. One can invite the other in: 'Dwell in me as I in you.' This is authentic, loving intimacy.

But you ask: How am I to withdraw the anima projection? By

46

what process do I come to the state of integrity and innocence that was mine before the fall? How does this interim marriage come about?

Ay, there's the rub. It isn't easy. It takes blood and tears and sweat and toil. Above all, it takes grace. For this is nothing other than the challenge of life lived authentically. If we live our lives in fidelity to ourselves and to God, if we are true to our innermost being, integration will somehow take place through our falls and risings, through our failings and successes, through our anguish and our joy, through our dark nights and our sunny days — and through that last dark night prior to death and joyful resurrection.

But in your case, since you have chosen celibacy, it will only take place through the process of contemplative prayer in which you are silently open to love and grace. You must remember the *nada, nada, nada* of St John of the Cross and the *mu, mu, mu* of Zen. You must remember that unless you renounce everything you possess you cannot be the disciple of Jesus. This is the contemplative process. Slowly, ever so slowly, projections and masks and fears and anxieties and addictions fall away. The little foxes die or scamper off into the dark night. Let them go. Let everything go. And you become your true self.

And as you let go, there arises from the centre of your being the blind stirring of love, the living flame of love, the divine fire. This is a pure gift of God: it is nothing other than the indwelling Holy Spirit. It is the love of Jesus going out to the whole world, to every man and woman, to the seas and the plains, to every blade of grass, to every grain of sand, and to the whole wide universe. You will be conscious that it is not your love, that it does not come from your ego. 'It is no longer I who live but Christ lives in me.' 'It is no longer I who love but Christ loves in me.' The Spirit joins himself to my spirit and cries out 'Abba Father.' Deep indeed is this love, liberated from the chains of possessiveness, anger and anxiety. It is what the old authors called chaste and perfect love.

When two people filled with the Spirit of love meet, then Spirit meets Spirit. This, I believe, happened when Elizabeth met Mary. Then Jesus met John the Baptist. The infant leaped in Elizabeth's womb and Mary said: 'My soul doth magnify the Lord . . .'. This meeting of the Spirit in two persons creates the deepest friendship and leads to the most profound intimacy.

Now you may ask about the role of the body in such meetings or about the role of the senses and of sexuality. For clearly such friendship and intimacy is no platonic rejection of matter.

St John of the Cross writes that, at the pinnacle of the mystical life, 'the deep caverns of sense, once obscure and blind, now give forth, so rarely, so exquisitely, both warmth and light to their beloved.' The cavern is a symbol of the unconscious; and the saint seems to mean that the senses and the sexuality are — not annihilated, never that — but are transformed and transfigured by the divine fire that burns in the depths of one's being. The desert fathers spoke about the return to paradise, claiming that through contemplation one is brought to the state of integrity, of innocence, of original justice in which sense was subject to spirit and the whole person was harmoniously subject to God. St John of the Cross, following Christian tradition from of old, means even more than that. He writes poetically of the divinization of the whole person in the fire of love, a divinization in which nothing human is lost. O happy fault (*felix culpa*) which restored man and woman not only to the state of innocence but to a divine state of harmony and love!

From this it is clear that mystical friendship can exist either in married or celibate life. In both cases sexuality is transformed; but the celibate person chooses not to express this sexuality in the way appropriate to marriage. This is quite possible; for when the living flame of love becomes very strong, sexual passion falls into the background, becoming less demanding and losing its compulsive dimension.

And yet the struggle for chaste love is a great one. Consummate mystics have fallen headlong; and some have come to grief. In all this we rely on God's grace which gently leads us to states of consciousness which human reasoning cannot understand or fathom.

The psychological process by which sexual energy is transformed into spiritual power has been carefully studied in the East, particularly in kundalini yoga. Here human energy is conceived as a serpent lying coiled at the base of the spine. And the art of kundalini is that of bringing this energy up the spine through centres known as chakras, until it reaches the crown of the head where it breaks out into great enlightenment. In this process sexual continence is much stressed: the energy may not be released through genital sexual activity. And all this is done in the context of meditation practised by the recitation of a mantra or awareness of the breathing or the use of visual imagery. Thanks to *Genesis* the serpent in Christian thought is wily and evil and slimy; but the serpent in kundalini is good and noble and life-giving — it is like the healing serpent that Moses lifted up in the desert.

Some Christians are studying kundalini, as I found when I visited Bede Griffiths' ashram in South India in 1984; but Christian research is still in its infancy. It seems to me that we Christians have much to learn from the study of energy — *prana, ki, chi, kundalini* — in Asian thought. For the fact is that in mystical prayer a fantastic energy is released, as is clear in the life of mystics like St Teresa. St John of the Cross speaks of fire, of flame, of wine, in an attempt to describe poetically this energy. He sometimes uses erotic language — but the relationship between spiritual energy and erotic energy is not yet clear. A study of kundalini might help us.

While the Latin tradition speaks little about psychic and spiritual energy, the Greek fathers have written extensively about the uncreated energy emanating from God, associating it with the light that emanated from the body and clothes of Jesus in the transfiguration. This could be an excellent starting point for dialogue with kundalini.

These are a few ideas that are going through my mind as I prepare my next book. I hope they will be of some use to you. Mystical theology has rightly been called the science of love. And in my opinion it is the science not only of divine love but also of human love. In the practical order I say that if you want to love deeply as a celibate you have to pray and fast. In this way you will be open to the Spirit in yourself and in others.

I've written enough; and I think it's time to visit the swimming-pool. I look forward to hearing from you again. Don't forget to pray for me lest after preaching to others I myself should be disqualified. Please give my greetings to John and to Mary. I hope I'll be able to see you all on my way to Ireland.

Keep smiling!

Bill J—————— S. J.

Santa Clara University
1 June 1989

Dear Ayako,

It was good to find your letter in my mail box and to know that all goes well with you. I miss Tokyo. If New York is the Big Apple, then Tokyo is the big something else — perhaps the big persimmon. Your description of the Emperor's funeral was impressive and I've been looking through the big picture-book you sent. Yes, the Japanese are a very aesthetic people (isn't it said that every Japanese is a poet?) with a fine sense of ceremony. I recall, believe it or not, the Tokyo Olympics in 1964 — how beautifully the opening ceremony was done! That was a turning-point when Japan, recovering from the Second World War, regained self-confidence and looked the world straight in the face. A lot has happened since then. As for the Emperor — I'm no rightist but I admire him a lot. It took courage to make the radio broadcast that brought the war to an end in August 1945. May he rest in peace!

Well, California here I come! I'm settling down at last. I always associate this part of the World with Aldous Huxley and his mescalin, Alan Watts and his beat Zen, Timothy Leary and his psychedelic trips — to say nothing of new religious sects, bogus mysticism, drug culture and all kinds of interesting, if spooky, things. I recall a cartoon showing a signpost pointing towards Nevada with the words: 'You are now leaving California. Resume normal behaviour.' I, however, have not had much time to view or indulge in abnormal behaviour. For I'm saddled with classes and interviews and writing — to say nothing of swimming and watching the blue sky.

One thing that has caught my attention, however, is the New Age movement which has now spread to the whole world. It began in California and is still particularly vibrant in Berkeley and San Francisco. It is a modern spirituality, claiming that we are on the verge of a new era and are developing a new consciousness. It borrows from gnosticism, alchemy, astrology, Hinduism, Taoism

51

in a somewhat eclectic way. While it is firmly opposed to all institutional religion it is open to mysticism everywhere. Among the Christian writers popular with New Agers are Meister Eckhart, Teilhard de Chardin, and Thomas Merton; but they are also open to *The Cloud of Unknowing*, St John of the Cross, and Padre Pio.

Browsing in a New Age bookshop I was impressed by the amount of literature written by doctors who have abandoned conventional medicine in favour of something more holistic. They seem to feel that orthodox Western medicine treats the symptoms without going to the roots of the disease — roots which lie deep in the psyche. And so they are exploring a new approach to the human body and to healing based on herbal medicines, acupuncture, acupressure, massage, all kinds of body work and the whole gamut of Chinese medicine. They are studying the flow of human energy through meridians and chakras. Of course I found a good deal of literature about kundalini. And there were some books about Fatima, Lourdes and St Teresa of Avila.

Together with a friend I visited a New Age exhibition in San Francisco. What an amalgam! Parapsychology was much in evidence: clairvoyance, clairaudience, telepathy, hypnosis, psychic healing, mind-reading, palmistry, psycho-kinesis, bilocation and the rest. Them rolfing and acupressure. Needless to say, there was a lot about meditation; and there were videos on Zen and yoga and Tibetan mysticism. Then astrology and Tarot cards and the I Ching and the prophecies of Nostradamus and Malachy. And one striking dimension of the whole exhibition was concern for the environment and for all that is green. Ecology seems to play a big part.

Of course I ask myself what is the authentic Christian attitude towards this New Age phenomenon. And no doubt you know my answer. Yes, dialogue! Of course I have found some Christians violently opposed to any dialogue with what they see as the occult and the demonic. Others, however, are open to dialogue; and a Catholic Magazine has devoted a whole issue to 'The New Age, a challenge to Christianity' featuring an article by a New York Jesuit who came to California to study the New Age and wrote a book about it. It may be true, of course, that this New Age movement contains traces of the demonic. But isn't that true of Christianity also? Jesus saw it clearly. 'Simon, Simon, behold, Satan demanded to have you, that he might sift you like wheat, but I have prayed for you that your faith may not fail . . .' (Luke 22:31). Jesus himself was tempted. Satan is everywhere. His presence need not obstruct dialogue; but we must be prudent and discerning, taking the wheat and leaving the chaff, appreciating the good and rejecting the evil, all the time offering the treasures of the Gospel.

The first question I ask myself is: Is there enough evidence to say that we are indeed at the threshold of a new age or a new era? Can we go on to say that the human family is developing a new consciousness?

Already in the 1960s the Second Vatican Council pointed a finger in that direction. It said that the human race is passing through a new stage of its history. It spoke of a crisis of growth, of transformation, of a new way of thinking, of a new attitude towards the world in which we live and even towards religion. It spoke of the unity of the human family and of a growing interdependence of men and women everywhere. It said that technology is transforming the face of the earth, that the human mind is broadening its dominion over time and space. And it urged Christians to scrutinize the signs of the times. It elaborated a new vision of the Church as the people of God, committed to world peace, walking hand in hand with Jews and Muslims, Hindus and Buddhists and all men and women of good will towards a common goal. If we take all this seriously won't we find in ourselves a new consciousness?

Since the Council we see an upsurge of interest in prayer, in contemplative prayer — yes, let me use the word — in mystical prayer. The West realizes that she has lost her mysticism, that she is like that woman who, having lost her silver coin, lighted a lamp and swept the house and sought diligently until she found it. Will we re-find our mysticism? I think so. I'm pretty sure we will. Dialogue with Buddhism and Hinduism as well as with Orthodox Christianity will certainly help us on our journey to illumination. And will dialogue with the New Age help us also?

Closely allied to this search for mysticism is an awareness of the psychic world of the occult. This world was very much alive in medieval Europe which knew of a Dr Faustus who craved for occult power and trembled in terror as he waited for Mephistopheles to arrive and claim his soul: 'The clock will strike, the devil will come and Faustus must be dammed.' This was the world wherein Macbeth met the three witches — 'bubble, bubble, toil and trouble/fire burn and cauldron bubble' — and Hamlet saw the ghost of his father. It was the world of haunted houses and the banshee. And now in the 1990s, with renewed interest in parapsychology and religious experience, we begin once more to take this world seriously.

Yet another interesting development within Christianity is the charismatic renewal which burst into song shortly after Vatican II. Here Christian men and women entered into new forms of prayer guided by the Holy Spirit. Getting away from the old discursive meditation they sang and spoke in tongues; they laid healing hands on the sick; they danced in the Spirit. They praised the Lord with outstretched hands; they claimed gifts of prophecy; they revived the rite of exorcism; they cast out evil spirits. In short, they came in touch with the whole psychic world of good and bad spirits which a rationalistic Western culture had tried to blot out.

Yet another extraordinary and significant religious phenomenon of this century is the frequent alleged apparitions of the Virgin Mary. There have always been centres of devotion to Mary, like Lourdes in France, Guadeloupe in Mexico and Zaragoza in Spain. But with Fatima something new was born. Though the central message was the Gospel teaching of conversion of heart, a political dimension entered, with prophecies about the spread of communism and the conversion of Russia — together with secrets entrusted to the visionaries and apocalyptic signs in the heavens. And since Fatima, such alleged apparitions have multiplied. Even as I write, young people in Medjugorje claim that they see the form and hear the voice of the Mother of God calling the world to prayer, penance, reconciliation and peace — and promising a great sign on the sacred mountain. Some of the visionaries claim to have seen purgatory and hell and the devil. They ask everyone to recite the rosary daily and to fast.

And there are many, many more alleged apparitions. When I was in Baguio in the Philippines in 1985 I heard of apparitions of Mary and saw a small shrine built there in her honour. Then I returned to Japan and heard of a similar event in Akita. At Garabandal in Spain, visionaries said that the Madonna had promised a great sign for the whole world. In Ireland, at Ballinaspiddle, people saw statues moving; and near the Trappist monastery of Mount Mellary there were alleged apparitions. More recently there has been talk of a Marian apparition in Cairo; and in 1988 the claim was made that Our Lady had been seen in the Ukraine by no fewer than one million people.

These events have affected the consciousness of millions. Many link these signs to the political turmoil in central Europe, Russia and China. Others predict the end of the world or some cataclysm which will strike if men and women do not change their hearts. Jungians, too, set great store by these phenomena, claiming that something is stirring in the collective unconscious of humankind — that the visionaries are simple people in touch with the unconscious and formulating something we all long to see. All this is grist to the mill of the New Age.

But the Church is very, very cautious. For all her defects, the institutional Church is a wise old mother, wily as the serpent and simple as the dove, with centuries of rich, sometimes bitter, experience. She knows of the pious hysteria, the fervent foolishness and the downright nonsense that can accompany such alleged apparitions. She knows that at the end of the first millennium something like hysteria swept through Europe with wild predictions about the end of the world, fundamentalist interpretations of *Revelation* and all kinds of superstition. And she foresees that something similar may occur at the end of the second millennium. Besides, she knows that attachment to signs can be an escape from the anguish of dark faith. Why should people want signs from the heavens? They have Moses and the prophets. If they do not believe Moses and the prophets neither will they believe the spinning sun or an apparition from heaven. A wicked and adulterous generation looks for a sign. Blessed are they who have not seen and have believed.

So the institutional Church acts slowly. Ordinarily she ignores or opposes these phenomena, knowing that most of the alleged apparitions will quickly be forgotten: the cult will peter out and the pilgrimages will die a natural death. If, however, the apparitions refuse to go away, she scrutinizes them with the utmost care, submits them to rigorous scientific investigation, gets the expert opinion of psychologists, parapsychologists and medical doctors. And finally if they pass all the tests the Church may say — not that the Mother of God apeared on earth and delivered a message — but that it is a good thing to make pilgrimage to this place and pray there for healing, for conversion and for world peace in accordance with the Gospel.

You ask what I really think about all this.

Well, I sincerely hope that we are coming to an age of authentic mysticism within Christianity and within the world. Just as fourteenth-century Europe saw a flowering of mystical experience — and historians probe into the reasons for this — so the twenty-first century could see a similar flowering. Such mysticism would be greatly promoted by dialogue between the great religions. And I believe that in this growth Asia will play a privileged role. However, in the movements I have spoken about I see some real dangers.

Let me put it this way. I see three levels of reality that are operative in religious experience :

The phenomenal world
The psychic world
The world of pure faith

Authentic mysticism calls us to the world of pure faith which is the world of the void, the emptiness, the nothingness, when we are faced with God who is the mystery of mysteries and is like night to the soul. In this deepest of all religious experiences there are no voices, no visions, nothing to cling to. 'Blessed are those who have not seen but have believed.' And yet this night is full of joy and is of such richness that the mystics speak of it as spiritual espousals and spiritual marriage — leading through death to the vision of God.

Then there is the psychic world. This is the world of voices and visions and miracles. It is the world of clairvoyance and telepathy. It is the world of psychic healing. It is also the world of the occult — of good and evil spirits. It can be a stormy yet fascinating world.

Now it is good that we should acknowledge the existence of this psychic world. Its reality is manifested not only in the New Testament but in the scriptures of all religions. To deny it would be to run counter to the experience of millions throughout history.

But (and this is the point I want to make) involvement in this world can be a snare and a trap. Just as in outer space there are black holes, so in this psychic world there are bottomless pits of deceit. Quite apart from the danger from forces of evil, there is the snare of attachment to psychic powers. Was not this the temptation of Simon Magus who wanted to buy these powers from the apostles? Was not this the temptation of Dr Faustus who sold his soul to the devil? These powers are very, very fascinating — much more fascinating than money or fame or political power.

Even if one does not go to the length of Simon Magus or Dr Faustus, one's progress can be obstructed by a somewhat innocent attachment to gifts of healing and the like. Then we need to remember the New Testament. We need to remember how some will come to theMaster saying that they worked miracles, cast out devils and did all kinds of wonderful things. And the Master will say: 'Amen I say to you, I know you not.' Again, people may speak in the tongues of men and of angels and they may have prophetic powers and they may have faith that moves mountains; but if they have not love, where does it all lead? Again, the seventy returned with joy because even the demons were subject to them and Jesus made the astounding comment: 'I saw Satan fall like lightning from heaven.' And then he went on: 'Behold, I have given you authority to tread upon serpents and scorpions, and over all the power of the enemy; and nothing shall hurt you. Nevertheless do no rejoice in this, that the spirits are subject to you; but rejoice that your names are written in heaven' (Luke 10:19).

From all these texts it is clear enough that psychic gifts may be given by God but one must not rejoice in them. One must not cling to them. And how difficult this is!

Now in the New Age movement I see an exaggerated emphasis on these psychic powers. This is no reason to reject dialogue. But it is a reason why, in dialogue, we can offer the New Age the authentic teaching of the Gospel. We can point the way to true faith and to the most profound religious experience.

But why do I speak about the New Age? Within our own household plenty of men and women are claiming to have psychic gifts. In our time we see people who hear voices, see visions, work miracles, claim the gift of prophecy, heal the sick and cast out evil spirits. I do not say these people are all phoney or inauthentic. I do not say they are out to deceive the public. They may well have received genuine gifts from God. But I do say that they must listen to the voice of one who saw Satan fall like lightning from heaven and who said that we should rejoice that our names are written in heaven. And this applies not only to the psychics themselves but also to those who flock to hear them and to receive some visible sign from heaven.

One who is called to authentic mysticism must go through and beyond the psychic world. That is to say, one must listen to the voice (not now a sensible voice) of one who calls to total renunciation of all things, including psychic gifts. If one renounces all, one will find all. 'Seek ye first the kingdom of God and his justice, and all these things will be given to you.' In the modern Church we need a St John of the Cross. 'Nothing, nothing, nothing; and even on the mountain nothing.' We need dialogue with authentic Buddhist meditation which rejects all these phenomena. Only in this way can we move into the realm of true faith which is the void. Only in this way can we launch out into the deep and into the unknown.

As you can see, I'm enjoying California; but my thoughts are constantly in Asia. In fact all my dreams seem to take place in Japan. And China! What is happening there? Something is stirring in the whole world and who can deny that something like a new age is in the offing?

I hope your writing is going well. Be sure to send me copies of anything you write.

Keep smiling!

Bill J⎯⎯⎯ S.J.

PS   Another word about the New Age. I see great interest in former lives, in reincarnation, in voices from the past. Is there here a place for dialogue? I do not accept the doctrine of reincarnation; it does not seem to square with the Christian revelation. But what we can learn from the New Age is that the human memory is much more complex than we once thought. We are influenced (sometimes injured) not only by everything that happened since our conception and life in the womb but even by what happened to our ancestors. Somehow psychic characteristics are carried on; somehow voices from the past can be alive in us. That is why some Christians take great interest in the healing of the family tree. And all this fits with the Jungian notion of the collective unconscious. Over to you.

Dear Robert,

Your letter reached me a few days ago. Many thanks indeed. It brought back memories of our conversations during your retreat. You really went through a dark night and, it seems, you are still in it. I've a lot to say to you but first let me tell you about myself.

Several months have elapsed since I arrived in California — and every day is a good day. That's a Zen Koan: *Every day is a good day*. I recommend it for your meditation. Just keep it in your mind; turn it over; chew on it — until the time comes when you cry out in crazy and joyful enlightenment: 'It is true! Every day is a good day. There's no such thing as a bad day. Whoopee!' After all, it must be so. Every day was created by God — and he saw that it was good. Every day you are alive is a good day — because to be alive is good. But let me not give reasons. You need no reasons. It's just a fact of life that every day is a good day; just as Juliana was dead right when she said that all will be well and all will be well and all manner of things will be well.

So you see that I've had a spark of enlightenment; and I shout out from my gut: 'Every day is a good day.'

But coming to particulars, I assure you that here in California I am learning things about Buddhism I could never have learned in Asia. People here are making a serious study of eastern religions — translating classical texts and examining Buddhist practice. In Berkeley I met a seminarian who is writing a doctorate thesis on American Buddhism and has visited Buddhist centres throughout the US. He told me that just as Christianity is making great efforts to inculturate in Asia, so Buddhism is making great efforts to inculturate in the US. He said, moreover, that most of the leaders of the American Buddhist community are Catholics and Jews — serious people who are searching for deep religious experience and do not find it in their own religious tradition. What a challenge to us!

For the fact is, Robert, that we are superficial. Not you, but most

60

of us! Of course we are now beginning to teach a nice form of contemplative prayer: repetition of the mantra and entrance into contemplative silence. Very fine indeed. But have we yet succeeded in introducing people to the void — to the night of the soul? If a person comes to us and says: 'I want to reach the pinnacle of enlightenment, can you lead me there?' what do we answer? Do we say: 'Come and I will show you the way'?

Apparently we don't. But Buddhism does. And so, serious young people are drawn to the Zen meditation hall. Mind you I am not criticizing them for going to the Zen meditation hall. I'm simply saying that it's a challenge to us.

For in Buddhism there are three important stages of consciousness. The first stage is awareness of the phenomenal world — the world we see around us, the world of *samsara*. The second stage is awareness of the psychic world of spirits, of psychic powers and occult knowledge. The third stage is the world of enlightenment, the void, the emptiness. This is the world about which *The Heart Sutra* sings so powerfully.

Now in order to get to the third stage, to the world of enlightenment, one must go through the psychic world. One must not be deflected from one's goal by voices or visions or psychic powers even when these are charismatic gifts. Like Ulysses tied to the mast we must never be allured away by the sweet voices of these seductive sirens. Only in this way can we go through the psychic world to the vast world of enlightenment, of emptiness, of nothingness, of the void. For this is the world of pure faith.

And this doctrine is similar to that of St John of the Cross who puts all his chips on pure faith, naked faith, dark faith and tells us to put no trust in voice or visions or whatever.

Now let me pause to say that in the Catholic Church today preoccupation with this fascinating psychic world is one of our greatest dangers and one of the reasons why so many remain in abysmal superficiality. Today we hear of healers and prophets and visionaries and miracle-workers and mind-readers within the Catholic Church; and people flock to them for help and consolation. I do not deny that some of these people have a real charism. Nevertheless, if we run to them for help instead of turning to the Gospel and the sacraments — are we any different from those politicians who consult soothsayers before they board planes or give

61

talks? Let us remember that on that day many will say, 'Lord, Lord, did we not prophesy in your name, and cast out demons in your name, and do many mighty works in your name?' And what will the Lord answer? Let us remember that what matters is pure faith. Blessed are they who have not seen and have believed.

I think that much responsibility lies with pious directors. St John of the Cross thunders against naïve directors who manifest great esteem for the visions and locutions of their spiritual children. Such directors don't help. And history is there to tell us that holy men are particularly vulnerable when they meet pious women visionaries, as holy women are particularly vulnerable when they meet controversial, prophetic men.

Anyhow, the point I make is that tied to the mast we must go beyond the psychic world of seductive sirens to the realm of pure faith wherein lies true enlightenment. And here, of course, I mean faith in Jesus Christ and in the Father Who sent Him.

I'm afraid I've indulged in quite a tirade. I didn't intend to do that. Let me get to your letter.

It is true that you have suffered a lot over the past few years: you have been suddenly awakened from your dogmatic slumber. But can you deny that it has been a good experience? Can you not now see the real power of the cross? It seems to me that your present situation can only be understood in the light of your personal history. All is part of a path you chose a couple of decades ago when you picked up St John of the Cross and *The Cloud* feeling that they were talking a language you understood and wanted to hear. Let me describe the process in your life as you have told it to me.

You devoted many years to quiet, simple prayer with the repetition of a word or mantra and the relishing of the gospels. Soon you had a sense of God's presence within and around — a loving awareness with an expansion of consciousness. For many hours you sat silently in the lotus with deep peace. In the outer world you had storms and tempests but you had joy and consolation within. Sometimes torrents of joy. And yet you did have that humiliating addiction which would not go away in spite of all your efforts and confessions and what not. Next your prayer became dry (arid is the word used by the old masters), but you kept sitting. And then came the tempest, the upheaval, the earthquake. Of course it was triggered off by exterior troubles; but these outer failures and contradictions were not sufficient to explain the awful anguish you experienced when you woke one night from a deep sleep — it was as though a rush of energy or a fountain of water surged up within you — and you found yourself awake and trembling with great fear. And you could not get back to sleep.

In retrospect you can see that there was an awakening in two senses. Literally you were awake and were to suffer from insomnia for many months to come. Metaphorically you were awakened — for your true self, slumbering at the very core of your being, was rudely but marvellously awakened. But at the time you did not see that; you didn't understand what was happening. What terror!

And you met the right person. Quite unexpectedly but providentially she appeared, and you poured out your whole soul to her.

First there were your dreams. So many centred around awakening. The footsteps on the veranda and the knocking on the door. The sound of the bell. The striking of the clock. Awake and get out of your room! 'Behold I stand at the door and knock . . ..' 'Hark! my beloved is knocking.' Yet the person knocking at the door was not the beloved but a fearful intruder. And how frightening was the clock! You resonated with Dr Faustus. 'The clock will strike, the devil will come and Faustus must be damned.'

Now you can see that you were called out into the night to the world of emptiness, nothingness, timelessness, spacelessness. You were called to the void. You were like the infant called from the security of the womb to the vast unknown and cruel world. Yes, it was all a rebirth.

But it was also a death. You were like the person called from this familiar world to the vast unknown world beyond the grave. Don't we all know that death is birth and birth is death? The fact is that your true self was awakened within you, and as it surfaced it pushed up all kinds of repressed material that had lain hidden in your mind for decades. All that fear and anxiety welled up; your whole life back to the womb lay open before you; all the hidden trauma and concealed hurts were revealed. You felt you were disintegrating, that you could not cope, that you would break down, that all was lost.

But you did cope. You clung to the faith that Jesus was your Saviour. And you had someone who listened and listened and wisely told you to let the process take place — 'Don't fight God.' And you did let the process take place; and all was well. It was also good that you did your yoga, particularly the deep breathing, took long walks and watched your diet. Body and spirit really interact. Take my advice: in times of spiritual crisis, look after your body.

For all the time, growth was taking place. Indeed growth was your problem: the process of growth was causing your suffering. Healing was also taking place — and purification. You were letting go of all those addictions that tortured you and held you in chains. You grew out of that humiliating addiction. You grew out of the need for sleeping tablets. It seemed that all was well again.

But then came a new cycle of disturbance with renewed storms. And once again the real fear of the void, the emptiness, the nothingness, the isolation, the acute loneliness. 'Is this hell?' you asked yourself. Alone and isolated for ever. It was as though you were again drawn into a world beyond space and time — and this was very, very frightening. You were losing everything that formerly gave you support. Worst of all you seemed to lose your friends. It was not that they abandoned you or you abandoned them; it was simply that they could no longer give you support; they did not understand. In fact a process of purification was taking place within you, including a purification of your relationships.

And then a new development took place. There arose within you a new energy, an inner fire. And again this caused you all the anxiety of one who does not know what is happening, of one who is afraid of losing control, of one who is losing self confidence.

But let me tell you with a very traditional image what was happening and is still happening. You are the log of wood, all damp and soaked in water. When you woke up that night with the rush of energy, the fire was applied to that sodden log. But it did not seem like fire. No flames were emitted; but instead, black smoke belched forth and you saw all your ugliness. It was only much later, when a degree of purification had been achieved, that you experienced the burning fire. The log was aflame. It had become the living flame of love, the blind stirring of love. And this indeed was the divine fire.

And that is where you now stand. I realize that the inner fire often causes you great suffering and acute pain. I realize that you often doubt about its divine origin and ask — 'Is it really a divine fire or am I going crazy?' I realize that this divine fire is killing you. Only remember the words of St John of the Cross: 'In slaying you have changed death to life.' Of course the divine fire is killing you — but it will also bring life. For this fire is the Holy Spirit. Gradually, oh so gradually, through suffering and pain you will lose your little separated ego in order to find your true self in the Spirit.

So accept the inner fire, which is divine fire. It will guide you more surely than the noonday sun to where he waits for you, him you know so well. You will be tempted to reject this inner fire, to regard it as an enemy (just as you resented that intruder who initially banged on your door) and to make all efforts to get rid of it, but you will not be able to do so. It is the deepest thing in you; it is your true self set on fire by the Spirit. So accept it; go along with it; let it guide you. Surrender and you will discover that this is the Spirit of love.

And so while I sympathize with your suffering and anguished outcry, I also feel great joy and ask you to pray: 'For he that is mighty has done great things to me and holy is his name.' He really has done great things for you and will do even greater things. But you must learn to cry out with Paul: 'But far be it from me to glory except in the cross of our Lord Jesus Christ . . .' (Galatians 6:14).

For you are going through purgatory. This is the place (or should I say the state?) in which the dead are purified by the fire of divine love before entering into eternal glory. Yes, the inner fire you experience is precisely that. Purgatory is not pleasant; but it does bring great joy.

Next week I'm going to Lake Tahoe for a few days with a Jesuit friend. I wish you could come with us. The mountain scenery there is majestic but it seems that the ravages of air pollution have extended even to those heights, contaminating everything. It makes me mad! The way we are destroying poor Mother Earth. I become more green every day! And isn't it infuriating to hear people quoting *Genesis* to justify their plunder of the environment?

Please let me know how things are going with you. You are always in my prayers and I know I am in yours.

Every day is a good day!

Bill J———— S.J.

Dear Jack,

Apologies for my long delay in answering your letter. It was not from lack of interest. A letter to you has been going round and round in my head for the past week; but only now do I get down to pen and paper. I'm glad you are interested in Buddhism and that you are getting involved in the dialogue. Mark my words, a lot will come out of this dialogue not only for Buddhism and Christianity but for the whole world. We are witnessing what Bernard Lonergan calls 'the shift to interiority.' That is to say, we are looking inward, finding God in the very depth of our being. And in this movement to the inner world Buddhism will help us a lot.

In your dialogue with Buddhism remember what the Council says in its decree on ecumenism. First it emphasizes that there can be no ecumenism worthy of the name without a change of heart, a metanoia, a confession of our own sins. And secondly it says that we must come to understand the outlook of our separated brethren. 'Study is absolutely required for this, and should be pursued with fidelity to truth and in a spirit of good will.' Aren't those words truly inspired? The Council also urges us to eliminate with truth and fairness, words, judgements, and actions which do not respond to the condition of separated brethren and so make mutual relations more difficult.

I like the way in which the Council stresses fairness. Play the game! And what I want to say here is that this same principle must be applied to our dialogue with Buddhism and Hinduism. Let us play the game. Alas, some stalwart theologians think they do a service to God when they blackball Buddhism, calling it life-denying, pessimistic, self-centred, etc., etc. What about fidelity to the truth? What about the spirit of goodwill? These good men need conversion of heart. With Paul I say: 'I bear them witness that they have a zeal for God, but it is not enlightened' (Romans 10:2). What a wonderful gift is enlightenment!

*

But let me return to your letter. You ask about the self in Buddhism and about the non-self. This is no easy problem. The mystery of the human person is second only to the mystery of God. The Gospel speaks of losing your life to find your life, of being born again and so on; and these paradoxes make sense in the light of the Buddhist doctrine of losing yourself to find yourself.

I find useful the Buddhist distinction between the small self and the big self. The small self (in Japanese *shoga*) is the separate self, the isolated self, the ego. It is the self that we build up when we imagine that we are separated from God, from the universe and from other people. And this small, separate self is illusory. To build it up is what traditional Christianity has called pride. We build it up when we cling to money and fame and power. Such clinging centres us on an illusory ego; it makes us forget God and destroy ourselves.

The big self (in Japanese *taiga*) is the self that is no longer separate but is open to the universe, to all men and woman, and to God. It can also be called the universal self or the cosmic self. It is the same 'I' but now this I has an expanded consciousness which embraces all. When I lose the consciousness of separation and isolation in order to embrace the consciousness of the all, I am reaching a state that Buddhism calls emptiness and Christianity calls humility. Both spiritualities claim that emptiness or humility is the cornerstone and basis of the whole building. If you would come to enlightenment you must be empty or humble.

And this is a process. One must let go! Listen to Ignatius who in his *Spiritual Exercises* tells us to let go of all clinging to money and to fame and to a good name. Embrace poverty and humiliation, he says. Follow Jesus who emptied himself, taking the form of a slave and then, like Jesus, you will be exalted in the most wonderful enlightenment. 'Blessed are you when men and women revile you and speak evil of you for my name's sake. Rejoice and be glad . . . '

And so the challenge in life is to lose the small self and to find the big self which is also the true self. Let me say more about the process.

I'm afraid there is only one way to the true self: death. We must die! At the end, of course, comes biological death; but before that comes a death that is psychological or spiritual. The pages of the New Testament are filled with the necessity of death. 'Truly, truly, I say to you, unless a grain of wheat falls into the earth and dies, it remains alone; but if it dies, it bears much fruit' (John 12:24). And death means losing everything. And so the contemplative life you have chosen is a process of losing all, even unto death. All and nothing.

Chinese philosophy puts it well when it speaks of a twofold path: the way of personal effort and the way of non-action or *wu-wei*.

Personal effort means that you rid yourself of addictions. I use the word addiction rather than traditional words like attachment or clinging because I have just been reading Gerald May who points out that we are all full of addictions or compulsive needs. Chemical addiction is just one aspect of the human who can be addicted to tobacco, alcohol, money, power, fame, success, or a relationship or religious experience, or almost anything. And all these addictions enslave us, alienating us from our true self and taking us away from authentic love of God and neighbour. St John of the Cross, fighting fiercely against addictions in *The Ascent of Mount Carmel*, is particularly radical when speaking about addiction to religious experiences such as visions, revelations, locutions and consolations of all kinds. 'Nothing, nothing, nothing, and even on the mountain nothing.'

Doesn't it sound terrible? But it is the royal road to freedom, to joy, to enlightenment and to the true self. 'Now that I least desire them', writes the Spanish mystic, 'I have them all without desire.' And this is an echo of Paul: 'Having nothing yet possessing all things.'

But human effort alone will not liberate us, particularly when the addictions are lodged deeply in the unconscious mind and heart. When we are driven violently by unconscious passion, 'I will' and 'I won't' are singularly ineffective and can even be counter-productive.

And so the other complementary path, the way of non-action (*wu-wei* in Chinese) is of primary importance in the contemplative life. Let me say a word about this way.

When one enters the contemplative path one may at first experience a gentle inner sense of presence. One senses that God is dwelling within or around and one can relax in his loving embrace. As time goes on, this sense of presence may become a blind stirring of love (the terminology is that of *The Cloud*) or a living flame of love. Again, this living love is at first gentle, sweet and consoling.

But if you persevere, the time may come when this stirring of love becomes a raging fire, a powerful surge of love energy which possesses your whole being and even knocks you for a loop. It can be very, very disturbing to feel that you are losing control, being taken over by another inner force. And so you cry out: 'What is happening to me? What is happening to me.' You may be overcome with fear.

'Fear not', says Jesus. 'I am.' This powerful energy that wells up within you is the Holy Spirit. Yes, the Spirit is burning out all your addictions, liberating you and killing you. Yes, killing in order to give life so that with St John of the Cross you will cry :

'In slaying you changed death to life.'

The little separate ego is killed and the new self, the real self comes to life in the Spirit. As Paul says, the Spirit joins himself to our spirit and cries out: 'Abba, Father.' So now you have found *your true self in the Spirit.*

As I said, the action of the Spirit can be frightening, unsettling, even violent. Remember the words of Jesus: 'From the days of John the Baptist until now the kingdom of heaven has been coming violently . . .' (Matthew 11:12). The action of the Spirit can have disturbing repercussions on the body — St John of the Cross talks of dislocation of the bones — and even more disturbing repercussions on the psyche. Sometimes you will ask: Is this the Spirit or am I going crazy? Is this love or is it some frightening psychic energy that has been released and is driving me insane?

This is the time when faith will be your support. Don't be afraid. Jesus will come walking on the waters and he will calm the storm. Have faith in him and in the scriptures and in the Christian contemplative tradition. With faith you will sing with the psalmist: 'Even when I walk through the valley of the shadow of death, I fear no evil; for thou are with me.'

I call this the way of non-action because in it you must give up all effort in order to surrender to the process. Let the process take place. Let growth take place. Don't fight against God. You are

70

privileged, and it is precisely the immense love of God which like an inner fire is making you suffer. So surrender to love.

Of course the key Christian question is: What is the relationship between the true self and God? Buddhism seems to stop at the true self without asking about the mysterious reality beyond. But Christians must ask about God.

And in the orthodox Christian tradition (as in the orthodox Jewish and Muslim tradition) human beings cannot say: 'I am God.' Neither can they say: 'I am separate from God.' Christian tradition, however, speaks constantly of union with God and being one with God. And in the scriptures John and Paul speak of indwelling. 'Dwell in me as I in you,' says Jesus. And Paul prays for the Ephesians that Christ may dwell in their hearts through faith. But what is this indwelling?

I think it is experienced in the Eucharist. Here we believe that the Risen Jesus who is divine and human is present within, transforming us into himself. While we change ordinary bread into ourselves, the bread of life changes us into itself so that we become Christ. In a sense we lose ourselves to become him. This is a union of love.

Now I believe that the loss of self to become the Eucharist is a fact of experience. I believe that many simple persons, after receiving holy communion, experience within themselves the fire of divine love; and they lose themselves in order to become this fire which is Jesus himself. And yet while becoming him they remain themselves. When Paul said: 'I live, now not I, but Christ lives in me,' Paul remained Paul and yet it was not his life but the life of Jesus that was vibrating within. St John of the Cross ties himself up in knots while trying to explain this text: 'In saying, I live, now not I, Paul meant that, even though he had life it was not his, because he was transformed in Christ, and it was divine more than human. He consequently asserts that he does not live, but that Christ lives in him. In accord with this likeness and transformation, we can say that his life and Christ's were one life through union of love.'

Whatever about theory, the experience itself is very real and very simple. And this is the glory of the Eucharist. The divine fire burns within and we become the fire as the logs become the flame. Yet

71

in becoming the fire we do not lose our personality. Michael or Margaret are transformed into Jesus and become Jesus. Yet Michael remains Michael, and Margaret remains Margaret.

Teilhard de Chardin throws some light on this when he distinguishes between absorption and union. In absorption I lose myself totally in the other, while in union I become the other while remaining myself. And surely some such union takes place in the great mysterious experience of receiving the Eucharist. I believe that ordinarily reception of the Eucharist will be an experience of faith, perhaps cold and blind faith. But there are times in the lives of some people when through devout reception of the Eucharist they lose themselves totally in the inner fire of love that has been enkindled within — and yet they remain themselves. They lose themselves and find themselves.

And through the Eucharistic Jesus we become one with the Father as Jesus was one with the Father. In other words we enter into the Trinitarian experience of Jesus who said: 'I and the Father are one,' who said that the Father was dwelling within him. Through the Eucharist we can make these words of Jesus our own. With the mystics we can speak of the 'divinization' of the human person or (if you prefer the other terminology) of the divinization of the true self through love.

In the Christian life we lose ourselves through love. But there is another loss of self which, for want of a better word, I call metaphysical. This loss of self takes place when we get an intuition of the unity of being and cry out: 'Being is' or 'Not a thing is.' This is the nothing or *mu* of Zen. And the whole Zen practice as well as the Zen *koan* are leading to this enlightenment.

A good example of this is found in the story of Hung-jen (AD 601–674) the fifth Chinese Zen patriarch. Seeing that his life was drawing to a close and wishing to choose a successor, the wise old man asked his disciples to write a poem that would express their degree of enlightenment. Whereupon the most promising disciple, Shen-hsiu wrote :

The body is the Bodhi tree
The mind is a clear mirror standing

72

Strive to polish it always
Let no speck of dust cling

This describes the process of Zen. Sitting in the lotus and letting go of everything you are wiping the mirror until it becomes totally clear and transparent. A fine description. But the poem was not accepted by the Master.

The right of succession was conferred upon a poor boy called Hui-neng who was washing dishes in the scullery. He wrote :

There is no Bodhi tree
There is no clear mirror standing
From the beginning not one thing is
Where then can a speck of dust cling?

Where then can a speck of dust cling? With this poem Hui-neng, the scullery boy, was effectively saying 'Nothing', 'Mu' — 'From the beginning not one thing is.' And this, the authentic Zen experience, delighted the heart of the old Master. What is this experience of nothing?

I believe that the experience of nothing is the same as the experience of everything. That is why we can say that all is nothing and zero equals infinity: 'Not a thing is' and 'All is' are the same experience. And in both one experiences the loss of the ego.

Let me illustrate this with another *koan* which runs as follows :

In the Sea of Ise
Ten thousand feet down, there lies a single stone
I will pick up that stone
Without wetting my hands

This is one of my favourite koans and I gave it to my students here in California. 'How am I to pick up that stone without wetting my hands?' I asked.

Their answers were incorrigibly Western. One student suggested scuba diving. Another said he would wear gloves. Another suggested using some machine or gadget to get the stone up without wetting the hands.

73

Then I gave my solution. I said that the Sea of Ise is my consciousness. The mysterious and beautiful stone is my true self. How do I pick up the stone? By sitting silently in the lotus and letting it emerge. 'Sit!' I said. 'Your true self will come to the surface and you will be enlightened beyond all subject-object duality. And, of course, your hands will not get wet.'

A student came to me after class. He had been too shy to speak up. Here was his solution :

> *There is no sea of Ise*
> *There is no stone to be picked up*
> *There are no two hands*
> *From the beginning not a thing is*
> *So how can the stone be picked up?*

I laughed when I read this. Was this the successor to Hung-jen? Did the scullery boy have the right answer? Is he the enlightened one? Or is the whole thing a hoax and a gigantic leg-pull?

From all this it is clear that the Christian loss of self through love and the Zen metaphysical loss of self are not the same. But they are complementary. I think the ideal for Christians is to have both religious conversion by which we are divinized through love, and intellectual conversion by which we are united with all in wisdom.

I think I've said enough. Over the past few weeks our eyes have been glued to the television watching the earth-shaking events in Tienanmen Square. What is happening in the world? Something is stirring in the hearts of men and women everywhere. I believe that all are demanding that their human dignity be respected. They will not tolerate oppressive regimes like Moscow and Beijing. A similar spirit animates the women's movement. Women, too, are demanding that their human dignity be respected. They will no longer tolerate systems that trample on them. And the same holds true within the Catholic Church. Theologians and writers are demanding that ecclesiastical authorities respect their human dignity. It's a great world. The action of the Spirit is palpable.

*

I look forward to hearing from you soon. Your letters always inspire me. Please remember me in your prayers and be sure of a remembrance in mine.

Bill J———— S. J.

Dear Betty,

Many thanks for your letter. I was glad to hear that you are taking classes in tai'chi. Of course you will be able to continue your practise when you come to Japan. To become an adept takes twenty years, they say. But don't get discouraged. Tai'chi brings youth and longevity; and in twenty years you'll still be a youngster (smile). Anyhow, in the parks and open spaces all over China you can see the people, old and young, fat and thin, short and tall, clad in traditional Chinese garb, practising tai'chi with grace and dignity. For me it is always a thrill to stand on the roof of Wah Yan College, Kowloon, watching them. The important thing in tai'chi is to let the energy (*chi* or *ki*) flow through your body giving strength and suppleness. The centre of the body is the *hara* or lower abdomen. This, in Japanese, is called *kikai* which means 'sea of energy'. If you can hold your strength in the *hara* you will experience an exhilarating sense of oneness.

In your letter you ask about Jesus in Asia. Is Jesus known and respected in China and Japan? And the answer is a resounding yes. Let me assure you that throughout Asia (and this includes the Islamic world and India) I have found the greatest esteem and reverence for Jesus. 'Whom do men say that I am?' is indeed an archetypal question asked by millions of people. Who was Jesus? Who is Jesus? The Catholic novelist, Shusaku Endo, has written a life of Christ, which is something of a best-seller in Japan. So many people are asking about Jesus.

Before coming to Japan I suggest that you read Endo's novel *Silence*. I myself translated it and I'll send you a copy. Quite honestly my reason for translating it was simply that I felt a great need to improve my Japanese. I was living with the words I had learned up to ten years previously and wanted to increase my vocabulary.

I had learned translation of Latin texts while at school in Liverpool. My Latin teacher (a famous Jesuit called Joe Woodlock) taught us a wonderful methodology: to read the text again and again and again, to read it aloud without a dictionary — to let the rhythm of the sentences and the music of the words flow into us. Only at the last reading could we use a dictionary (and then it usually wasn't necessary because the right word suggested itself) before sitting down and rapidly writing out the whole.

And I followed this methodology with *Silence*. Each day I read two pages, listening to the text on a tape-recorder, again and again and again. I felt the flow of the sentences; and, above all, the spirit of the author was entering into me. And then I wrote it out spontaneously. If I may say it modestly, I think the translation was well done. It flows smoothly and I like it.

But the content of the book! A colleague of mine in Sophia says it is like the Rorchact blots: everybody takes his or her own interpretation. I, like an innocent lamb, agreed to translate the book before reading it. Later I found myself in a hive of controversy.

The novel is about a Portuguese missionary who comes to Japan during the turbulent Christian century and ends up by trampling on the crucifix as a sign of apostasy. He does this terrible thing after weeks of agonizing discernment in a Japanese prison. And he is motivated not by fear of the frightening torture to which he will be subjected but from love of his people, to save them from the horrendous suffering of being suspended upside down in the sulphur pits of Unzen. The hero goes through a dark night of the soul because of God's silence; and he asks: Why? Why? Why? Why does God not speak to us?

The author is obviously sympathetic towards the missionary — who gives up evangelization as a useless task. At the back of Endo's mind is the conviction that institutional religion cannot take root in the swamp of Japan unless it undergoes a radical transformation. His book is finally a desperate plea for Christian adaptation to Japanese culture.

But (and this is my point here) it is quite clear that while institutional Christianity in its traditional form does not fit Japan, Jesus does. The apostate missionary has a great love for Jesus and is motivated solely by this love. It is precisely love for Jesus that prompts him to trample on the crucifix. And Endo himself clearly loves and respects Jesus in a remarkable way. Indeed one who reads his books cannot help being impressed by the author's fascination with the personality of Jesus. Jesus, he writes, is looking over his shoulder as he works. The peripheral aspects of Christianity do not interest him. His central problem is: 'Whom do men say that I am?'

But the book is gloomy. There is no let up. The missionary struggles and struggles. And when I came towards the end of my translation I fell into something like depression.

I think I've said enough about *Silence* but since I've introduced it to you, let me complete the saga.

When I finished the work I couldn't find a publisher. The book went the rounds; but nobody was interested. And so we published it in Sophia. And then something happened. Graham Greene chose it as his book of the year in one of the big Sunday papers. And what a difference that made! Immediately from the whole world came requests for translation rights — from Poland and Denmark and Norway and every imaginable country. Now the book is in Penguin, and Endo is a potential Nobel Prize winner. But I will translate no more of his books. I find them too disturbing.

Sometimes Zen Masters refer to the Gospel and to Jesus with remarkable insight. A few years ago a Zen Master gave a retreat to Christian monks in the US, and his principal koan was the death and resurrection of Jesus. What wisdom we would have if we could break through to enlightenment with that koan! And if you want to see how Zen throws light on the Gospel read *Zen and the Bible* by my friend and colleague Kakichi Kadowaki.

Further afield in India we find Mahatma Gandhi. At first he was fascinated by the Sermon on the Mount and its teaching of non-violence. But towards the end of his life it was the person of Jesus that drew him. The only picture on the wall of his tiny room was that of Jesus; and in Rome he wept before Michelangelo's dead Jesus in the arms of his mother. Many more examples could be quoted.

In my old, unenlightened days I did not take these people seriously. Almost unconsciously I said to myself: What do they know about Jesus? To know him one must be a Christian. Alas for my ignorance!

For the Council says well that by his incarnation the Son of God has united himself with every human being. He is Lord of the people of God which consists of Christians holding hands with Jews and

Muslims and Hindus and Buddhists and all men and women of good will. Furthermore, after speaking of the mystery of redemption, the Council makes this beautiful comment: 'All this holds true not only for Christians but for all men and women of good will in whose hearts grace works in an unseen way.' And it further says that 'in a manner known only to God' the Holy Spirit offers to every man and woman the possibility of being associated with the Pascal mystery.

In short, Jesus belongs to the whole human family. Remember how Paul accepts even those who preach Christ from envy and rivalry. 'What then? Only that in every way, whether in pretence or in truth, Christ is proclaimed; and in that I rejoice' (Philippians 1:18). Let us not monopolize him. A friend of mine in Asia keeps saying: 'Jesus belongs to everyone. Don't Christianize him too much!' He is the archetypal man. He intercedes for all. He died for all. He is working in the hearts of all. Everyone has a right to speak about him.

A colleague of mine in Sophia University asked his young students, most of whom were agnostic or Buddhist, to write an essay on 'my Jesus.' He was astonished at the beautiful reports he received. Of course you may say that these moving essays were just the idealistic dreams of kids who knew nothing about the real Jesus. But I prefer to believe that grace was working in their hearts in an unseen way and that, in a manner known only to God, the Holy Spirit was offering to them the possibility of being associated with the Pascal mystery.

And by way of corollary let me ask a further question: Just as Jesus belongs to the whole human family can we say that the Buddha belongs to the whole human family? For just as Zen masters comment on the gospels and speak about Jesus, so Christians are giving Zen-style retreats and speaking about Buddhism. Yes, I believe that some committed Christians have profound insight into the Buddhist sutras, insights that will help Buddhism in its growth towards maturity. The Buddha and the Buddhist patriarchs belong to the whole human family and will surely contribute to the religious growth of all men and women.

And so, Betty, please come to Asia prepared not only to learn tai'chi, not only to learn about Buddhism but also to learn about Jesus. Christianity has a great future in that continent. Already, millions of Asians are committed to Jesus even though they have made no commitment to an institutional church. More and more I see Asia creating its own theology and finding a new and brilliant understanding of sacred scripture. Remember that the Asian peoples are deeply contemplative; and the Council spoke of a growth in the understanding of scripture through the contemplation of the faithful who, like Mary, ponder these things in their hearts. Won't Asian contemplatives give us an understanding of scripture the West has not dreamt of?

Perhaps Asia will ask for perestroika within the Catholic Church — for new structures that will suit Asian civilization and culture. This is the plea of writers like Shusaku Endo. And everyone who knows China says that some measure of autonomy must be accorded to the people who comprise one-fifth of the world's population.

I'm preparing to leave Santa Clara for Ireland, stopping off at Reno and New York. It has been good here. Two things I enjoyed a lot were the swimming-pool and the piano. When I was a kid the piano was a central piece of furniture in the house and I still turn spontaneously to it for relaxation and inspiration.

Give my greetings to Frank. I'm glad his Buddhist studies are going well. He asked about the limits of compromise. Tell him to read and meditate on the Decree on Ecumenism which speaks about a 'hierarchy of truths'. That will give him a clue. I'll write to him as soon as I get to Ireland.

Keep smiling and God bless both of you.

Bill J———— S.J.

PS I know you are not crazy about Zen; but I'll give you a Zen saying for your pious rumination :

Sitting, only sitting
And the grass grows green by itself

Just sit. You don't need to worry about the grass. That's not your problem. Not a single snowflake falls in the wrong place. Not a sparrow falls to the ground without permission of your Father. Just sit without preoccupation or anxiety. 'Thy will be done on earth as it is in heaven.' Let God act. Don't fight God. But, you say, He will kill me? Yes, you must die. The New Testament says so again and again. But you will rise again, even in this life, and your joy no one will take from you.

Dear Frank,

I write this letter in a coffee shop in Grafton Street in the centre of Dublin. Quite different from the Tokyo coffee shops — though the price of a cup of coffee is about the same! Here there is no sweet and delicate music but a lot of noise, and the place is full to overflowing. I'm sitting at a table with three vivacious Irish colleens who are talking and laughing and puffing cigarettes and blowing the wretched smoke into the air. However, it doesn't bother me too much. Outside in the street dishevelled musicians are playing a mixture of rock and traditional Irish melodies. Then round the corner is the Carmelite church with plenty of good people saying the rosary or praying before the Blessed Sacrament. All in all I love the atmosphere of Grafton Street. I suppose it appeals to the Irish Bohemian in me. Anyhow, let me get to your letter.

I'm glad your studies are going well. Buddhism is really fascinating isn't it? But your question floored me. You ask me to describe the Zen enlightenment or awakening, known as satori. Ha! Ha! Frank, how naive can you be? I won't attempt to describe satori in Zen, much less the great awakening of the Buddha himself; but I will tell you what I myself understand by enlightenment and how one comes to it.

It seems to me that in the Christian way to God there are two (at least two) important religious experiences. The first is conversion or *metetanoia*. This was the experience of Paul when he was blinded by that unearthly light and fell to the ground. Paul's life was revolutionized. He suffered the loss of all things, as he himself says, and he began a new life.

The second is enlightenment. This was the experience of Paul when, as he relates in the Second Letter to the Corinthians he was caught up into Paradise — whether in the body or out of the body he did not know, God knows — and he heard things that cannot be told, which man may not utter. Whereas on the road to

82

Damascus Paul repudiated his past life, in this second experience he went forward on the road already chosen.

And I believe that these two movements can be found in the Christian life. There is the conversion experience in which we repudiate our sinful past; and as the way of purgation never ends, so this also never ends. And there is the awakening by which we advance in wisdom and love. Needless to say we don't go as far as Paul (some theologians held, erroneously I think, that he had the beatific vision), but we can follow in his footsteps. We can grow towards enlightenment.

Being a dyed-in-the-wool Jungian, I used to say that the goal of human life is individuation whereby one comes to discover one's true self. I linked this with the famous saying of Irenaeus that the glory of God is man and woman fully alive. While I still regard this as a beautiful approach to human life, I now prefer to say that the goal of human life is enlightenment. This enlightenment is a process of spiritual growth whereby I become the Jungian wise old man, but (and this is important) the process only reaches fruition through death and resurrection and the vision of God. In short, the great enlightenment, the goal of human life, is the vision of God.

By vision I do not mean that we look at God as we might look at a picture. I mean union with God, becoming one with God. The old theologians said that in this life we can be united with God according to the will — that is to say, by love — but only in the next life can we be united with God according to the intellect; that is, by vision. I need not here go into the theological controversy as to whether the vision of God is granted to some in this life. Enough to say that I myself hold by the Johannine text that no one has ever seen God.

But all the mystics agree that we can have foretastes of the beatific vision. There can be moments when God pierces the cloud of unknowing with a ray of spiritual light, revealing to us great secrets of his glory. There can also be an enduring gift of high wisdom by which we know God in a wonderful way. And this I call enlightenment. What, then you ask, is the way to enlightenment?

An important text is that of St John who says that the one who loves knows God. 'The one who does not love does not know God; for God is love' (1 John 4:8). Note that John does not say that the one who studies theology knows God. Needless to say the theologian is not excluded; but the epistle stresses that the way to enlightenment is love.

So love is the way to Christian enlightenment and there is no other. This love has a twofold thrust: love of God and love of neighbour. In either case it is ecstatic. That is to say, my consciousness expands and I go out of myself — I go out to all men and women who have ever lived or ever will live, to the whole material universe of moons and stars and planets, to every blade of grass and every grain of sand, to every living creature, and to the great mystery at the centre of all, the great mystery we call God — and God is love.

Now this loving expansion of consciousness leading to enlightenment and supreme wisdom takes place in people who devote their lives to the poor and the sick and the oppressed and to the service of others. But it also takes place when we sit in meditation. For when we sit in silent contemplative prayer, sooner or later, there arises within the heart the blind stirring of love, the living flame of love, the inner fire, the loving energy of the Holy Spirit. And this love leads to the highest wisdom in fulfilment of the words of Scripture that the one who loves knows God.

So this is the path to enlightenment. It is a path of great joy, when you will sing like a troubadour: 'This guided me more surely than the light of noon to where he waited for me — him I know so well.' I have told you in the past that this path has a twofold thrust so that we can speak of the way of personal effort and the way of non-action. Now let me add that the way of non-action assumes increasing importance as we go on. This is the way of suffering, of undergoing, of accepting. For this inner fire, besides giving high and perfect wisdom, also weeds out addictions and pulls up the roots of sin, a process which can be very painful. But it guides us more surely than the light of noon to where he waits for us — him we know so well.

Where is it guiding me? Where is he waiting for me, him I know so well? The answer is that it is guiding me to death — and through death I find him I know so well. Death means the loss of all things and the finding of all in God. It means that we lose our self and find our self. That is why the motif running through every description of this path is *all and nothing*. 'Alling and noughting' says the *Cloud*. 'Todo y nada' says St John of the Cross. 'Nothing,

nothing, nothing' says Zen. 'If a man offered for love all the wealth of his house it would be utterly scorned' (Ct 8:7).

I have said that this path of losing all things, including one's life, is the path of the Gospel. You will be helped in this path by silent sitting in which you are attentive to the inner flame and let go of all things. You will also be helped by reflecting on certain prayers.

One such prayer is the *Take and Receive* of St Ignatius. Here we offer everything to God. We offer all and keep nothing. 'Take, O Lord, and receive my memory, my understanding and my whole will, whatever I have and possess . . .' This is the giving all to remain with nothing. But we receive all when we continue to pray: 'Give me thy love and thy grace, for this is enough for me.' All and nothing.

The prayer of prayers is the *Our Father*. Recite this prayer slowly again and again. You will see that here there is no ego. We pray that God may be glorified, that God's kingdom may come. We pray that he may give us, not me, our daily bread. As you recite this prayer you will find that you are losing your ego and that your eyes are opening to the vision of God in all things.

Such is the path to enlightenment. A couple of years ago we held a Buddhist-Christian symposium in Sophia University in Tokyo. I gave a paper on enlightenment in St John of the Cross, showing that his path is quite similar to that of Buddhism. When I had finished speaking, a participant raised his hand and asked about the role of Christ. He said the whole process could take place without Christ and he didn't see why I had to bring Christ into it at all. To this I answered that for St John of the Cross Christ was all. His whole doctrine was based on love for Christ and love for the Gospel. Without Christ everything would fall to the ground.

My answer was, I believe, correct. However, only afterwards, as happens so often, did I think of the further explanation I should have given to my questioner. From my faith I know that Christ is the very centre of this path. It is not something I can prove to someone else by dialectic or by psychological reasoning. I begin this journey by an act of radical faith in Jesus and in the Gospel. This act of faith penetrates the whole journey and the whole process. 'I live, now not I, but Christ lives in me.' If you say to me: 'Christ does not live in you, something else lives in you,' I cannot *prove* you wrong. It is my faith. So much for your query.

A couple of days ago I went to *Madame Butterfly* at the Gaiety. For me it is always a tear-jerker and of course it brings me back to the Japan I love. Some years ago I saw it on Japanese television with a Japanese maiden, trained in Italy, in the title role. That was magnificent. Here in Dublin Madame Butterfly herself was less attractive but the overall performance was very moving. 'One fine day . . .'. And the Dublin crowd was very responsive. There is here a good appreciation of art. I suppose you know that the Dublin audience was the first to recognise Handel's *Messiah*. They were the first to stand to attention for the Alleluia Chorus. James Joyce, Oscar Wilde, George Bernard Shaw, W.B. Yeats, Samuel Beckett — Dublin has its artists. I also saw *My Left Foot*, the story of the handicapped Christy Brown. But I didn't like it a lot. There was too much of the pub and the fighting and the stage-Irishman stuff. That puts me off.

Well, Frank, time is moving on, very quickly. Soon you and Betty will be in Japan and I hope to meet you at Narita. With Augustine I ask: What is time? Buddhism has a lot to say about time — about the cycle of birth and death — and it's worth studying. You'll find that as your meditation gets deep your sense of time changes; you may even find that you are somehow outside time. Meanwhile carry on with your study. Dumoulin's *History of Zen Buddhism* is well worth reading. Yes, Suzuki's *Zen Mind: Beginner's Mind* is good; I used it with my students. If you can find Ruben Habito's *Perfect Liberation* you'll get some new ideas. Let me know how your study is going. I enjoy your letters.

God bless you and Betty and the children!

Bill J.T.

86

PS Thanks to both of you for the colourful birthday card. It made me laugh. Yes, I feel fine. They say that a Zen Master's best years are between seventy and eighty. So haven't I a lot to look forward to?

Dear Frank,

I write this letter beneath the blue skies of Dublin. Yes, there seems to be something to this talk of global warming. The dark rainy clouds, they say, are vanishing and Ireland is developing a Mediterranean climate. Perhaps the tourist trade is behind it. 'Ireland of the blue skies, clear air and unpolluted water.' Anyhow I do find here a sense of Europe that is quite striking. The school kids are learning French and German, and going to the continent. At the mass for the late cardinal the prayers of the faithful were read in French, Spanish, German, Irish and English. Yes, English came last! I myself was reminded of my European dimension when I got a new passport: the old green booklet is gone and in its place is a maroon passport with 'European Community' written across the top and 'Ireland' underneath. History is moving on. But will the one Europe be a return to the old Christendom? Will there be a Christian continent from the Atlantic to the Urals? I doubt it. Unless, of course, you think of Christianity as 'the people of God'. In that case we can all be one — Jews and Muslims and Hindus and Catholics and Protestants and Orthodox and agnostics of good will. Ha! Ha! What an ideal!

Enough about Europe. Your interest is now in Asia. I liked your letter. I think you have reached the heart of the matter when you ask about cognitional theory and if there can be a Christian non-dualism or *advaita*. It is sometimes said that the East is monistic and the West is dualistic or that Asian religions are pantheistic. And of course this is nonsense. There is a lot of woolly thinking around. It seems to me that we must first search for a sound cognitional theory that will be acceptable to everyone. And on that we can build our theologies.

As you know, the central problem of Greek philosophy was 'the one and the many'. People of profound insight, the Greeks knew from experience that there is one thing and there are many things.

88

They had the experience, common enough, of the unity of being — an experience that sometimes comes to people in a flash: *all is one*. And they also had the common-sense experience that all is not one: there are many things. How to reconcile these two experiences was the problem of the one and the many.

Following Aristotle, Thomas solved this problem by saying that beings are one by reason of their existence, beings are many by reason of their essence — beings are one in *that they are*, beings are many in *what they are*.

Now this may sound like airy-fairy theory but the medieval mystics (many of whom were dyed-in-the-wool Thomists) made it practical in their teaching on prayer. The author of *The Cloud* tells his disciple to sit and be aware *that you are* and forget *what you are*. Just be. Just become aware *that you are* and *that God is*. Remember that God is your being — and this is a remarkable, Thomistic insight — and in Him you are your true self. And then the time will come when you must forget yourself to be aware only of the being of God. In this total self-forgetfulness you are aware of the complete unity of all being.

Now this way of contemplation is so similar to Zen that many Christian teachers of Zen appeal constantly to *The Cloud* and use it as a textbook. Just sit and be! Away with reasoning and thinking! Do not think about *what you are* and *what God is* but only *that you are* and *that God is*. Then in a practical way you will solve the problem of the one and the many.

In Zen, of course, the practical solution is *kensho* which means 'seeing into the essence of things'. One who attains to this experience loses self and, with great joy and gratitude, discovers that all is one. This *kensho* experience is of great value for Christians many of whom, with or without the guidance of a Buddhist master, have come to this beautiful enlightenment.

One attains to *kensho* either by silent, existential sitting or by wrestling with the *koan*.

In all this I have found the thought of Bernard Lonergan very helpful. Bernard maintains (and who could deny it?) that most people do not understand their own process of knowing. They think they are separated from the object they know. They think the object is 'out there' and they are having a good look at it. In fact, however, there is no separation: we are all one: the knower and the known are united in the greatest of all unions — Thomas speaks of the *unio omnium maxima*. And we only come to the knowledge of this oneness by an intellectual conversion, an inner revolution.

I myself see an undeniable similarity between the *kensho* of Zen and the intellectual conversion of Lonergan. But there is also a difference. For Lonergan goes on to show the objectivity of knowledge (in this he was answering Kant) and to propound his theory of moderate realism.

Again, this may sound like airy-fairy theory; but it is very practical and goes towards demolishing the old prejudice that the West is dualistic and the East is monistic. If any human being, east or west, lives in a truly authentic way he or she will come to experience the unity of all things while, at the same time, retaining the common-sense experience of the diversity of all things.

In the Christian life it is obviously of the greatest importance that we call out: 'Abba, Father'. This is the prayer the Lord himself taught. But the Lord's prayer must not lead us to think we are separated from God. Jesus who prayed 'Abba, Father', also said 'I and the Father are one'. We pray to the Father with whom we are one. Is not this the very core of the Christian paradox? And I believe we can only come to some understanding of this mind-boggling mystery by a consideration of love. To understand the Gospel one must probe not only the mystery of cognition but more importantly the mystery of love.

For besides intellectual conversion there is religious conversion wherein my being becomes being-in-love. This also is an experience which many people have and which in its most intense form is mysticism. Love, it will be remembered, is ecstatic — it goes out to all men and women, to the whole environment, to the mountains and the seas and the forests — and to God who is the source of all. When my being becomes being-in-love through religious conversion I discover the truly Christian non-dualism or *advaita*. God is love. And if God is love there can be no separation.

But let me look at Christian meditation in the context of non-dualism. Ordinarily one begins with the gospels in which a key question is 'Simon, son to John, do you love me?' and Peter's answer (which becomes my answer), 'Lord, you know all things, you know that I love you.' And this love grows and develops, leading to an indwelling whereby we dwell in Jesus as the branch dwells

90

the vine, and with Jesus we dwell in the Father.

This indwelling is of the greatest importance in the experience of Paul and John. 'As the Father has loved me, I have loved you, dwell in my love.' And it is experienced in the Eucharist. 'The one who eats my flesh and drinks my blood dwells in me and I in him.' Nor does the eucharistic Jesus simply dwell in us as water in a glass. His union with us is much more intimate; for we are transformed into him. In a sense I become Jesus. So much so, that the old authors spoke of identification with Jesus. And is not this non-dualism? In this context I recommend to you the little book *One with Jesus* by Paul de Jaegher. It is old now; but it remains a classic.

We become one with Jesus. And then as Jesus dwells in the Father we also, in Jesus, dwell in the Father. We, so-to-speak, enter into the heart of the Trinity.

And yet while becoming Jesus we remain ourselves. Indeed, we become our true selves. And here again we are faced with a great paradox of Christian mysticism. I become the other while remaining myself. Teilhard expresses it well when he says that union differentiates. When we are one with the other we are most ourselves. In this respect union differs from absorption wherein one loses oneself in the other.

Again, this is not airy-fairy theory. Many people experience this union quite powerfully in the moments after receiving holy communion. They experience the divine life flowing within them and becoming their life, yet they remain their unique selves. And the same holds true for interpersonal relations. If I am infatuated by another I become so engrossed in this person that I forget myself completely. But when my love becomes very, very deep I am united with the other while remaining myself and she is united with me while remaining her self. 'Jesus said to her, "Mary", she turned and said to him in Hebrew "Rabboni", [which means Teacher]' (John 20:16). And then Jesus said to her: 'Do not cling to me . . .'.

I have spoken of Christian non-dualism in the context of indwelling. The mystics speak of the same experience in the context of marriage and man-woman love; and from the time of Origen *The Song of Songs* has been something of a text book of Christian mysticism. And while pious Christians have frequently raised horrified eyebrows and wished that the erotic song of Solomon had never been written, people with mystical experience resonate with

91

it very easily, knowing that the ultimate sexual experience — to which other sexual experiences point — is union with God.

St John of the Cross, following a long tradition, speaks of spiritual espousals and spiritual marriage. The latter is 'a total transformation in the Beloved in which each surrenders the entire possession of self to the other with a certain consummation of the union of love. The soul thereby becomes divine, becomes God through participation, insofar as is possible in this life.' Here, indeed, is a very radical non-dualism. And the saint compares carnal marriage with spiritual marriage:

> Just as in the consummation of carnal marriage there are two in one flesh, as Sacred Scripture point out (Genesis 2:24), so also when the spiritual marriage between God and the soul is consummated, there are two natures in one spirit and love, as St Paul says in making this comparison: 'He who is joined to the Lord is one spirit with Him' (1 Corinthians 1:17).

After speaking about marriage, the saint goes on to explain his non-dualism with yet another striking figure :

> This union resembles the union of the light of a star or candle with the light of the sun, for what then sheds light is not the star or the candle, but the sun, which has absorbed the other lights into its own.

In the above theology St John of the Cross is attempting to put into human language an experience which is very simple and non-problematic. In the mystical life one is penetrated through and through with the flow of divine life. Needless to say, it is not a genital experience at all, but it is an inflow of God's love into one's very being so that there are 'two natures in one spirit and love'.

In *Method in Theology* Bernard Lonergan, writing about 'retreat from differentiation' says that 'it occurs in sexual intercourse when both partners undergo a suspension of individuality and fall back into a single stream of life'. And I believe that in mystical experience, at a completely different level, the human person undergoes a suspension of individuality and falls into the divine stream of life. And the great challenge of the mystical life is to surrender to that stream of divine life, a surrender which involves nothing other than death.

In the whole non-dualism debate between Christianity and Buddhism the *cogito* of Descartes is frequently quoted :

'I think, therefore I am'

After reflecting on this some Zen people have responded :

'I do not think, therefore I am not'

This is indeed a valid description of Zen. One abandons all thinking and arrives at the non-self position known as *muga*.

But I believe the Christian position could be stated as:

'I love therefore I am'

When I love authentically my 'I' becomes the true I, the true self, the cosmic self. This is the self that exists in God.

Or again the Christian position could be stated as :

'I am loved therefore I am'

Here I say that it is precisely because I am loved that I exist. I am, so to speak, loved into existence.

And in all this it is important to remember that there are two kinds of love. There is an active love wherein by an act of the will I go out to John and Jane and the universe and the all. But there is also a passive or non-objective love. This is like a fire that is lighted within and has no specific object although it does radiate to John and Jane and the universe and the all. Now my being is being-in-love. It does not go out to others by an act of the will but pours out like a fountain of water because it is the love of God Himself. This is the love that vivifies the contemplative life. This love is the core of mysticism.

As usual I've written more than I intended. I'm glad your preparations are going well. Yes, read *The Heart Sutra* again and again and again. It will carry you into the void. It's good also to read some Japanese history and to keep in touch with contemporary Japan. Things are changing very rapidly as Japan becomes the leading economic power in the world. Difficult to believe it is the same country I went to in the 1950s. Although Japan has such a reputation for affluence you will find that the people lead a very spartan life. They get up early and work hard. The tempo of life is very fast. In fact all over East Asia — in Korea, in Taiwan, in Hong Kong, in Japan — people work so hard that I wonder if the West will be able to compete economically. Who knows the future? Japan has been greatly influenced by Germany, and in the *Irish Times* I saw a picture of a huge chunk of the Berlin Wall displayed in a department store in Tokyo. I wonder what the Japanese are thinking about the reunification of Germany. I'll find that out when I get back.

Greetings to Betty and the children. You are always in my prayers.

Bill J.

Dear Frank and Betty,

Excuse me for lumping you together in one letter. This time I have the same thing to say to both of you; and doesn't *Genesis* say that the two shall be one? It was good to hear that your preparations are going well. Soon you will be in Japan. I recall the words of my Jesuit Rector when, as a young student, I was starting my study of philosophy. 'Now you are going', he said 'for what I might call a mental thrill.' It was a mental thrill, those three years in the bog. And I'd like to say the same about your visit to Japan. Let's hope it will be a mental and emotional and spiritual thrill.

Yes, I think you should go to Hiroshima. But more important than Hiroshima is Nagasaki. Don't miss Nagasaki. It's a long journey from Tokyo (though the *shinkansen* goes like lightning) and it's a journey into a different world. As you know, Nagasaki is in Kyushu, the southern island which first opened its doors to the West. It was here that Xavier stepped ashore in the sixteenth century, and it was here that the Dutch and English developed their trade with the famous or infamous black ships. It was here that Madame Butterfly sang her sad song — you can see the house where she supposedly lived and died, and sang her one fine day. It was here that most of the old missionaries lived and died heroically. Here thousands upon thousands of Japanese martyrs shed their blood or were suspended upside down over cruel sulphur pits; and here is the hill on which the twenty-six martyrs were crucified and died reciting the *Te Deum*: you can see their shrine close to the station. Here on Thursday, 9 August 1945, at two minutes past eleven in the morning, fell the second atomic bomb. It exploded over the cathedral where the Christians were attending mass; and none survived. The blood of the martyrs is the seed of the church; and you may find, as I have found, that Nagasaki is the only part of Japan where Christianity is really indigenous, really part of the landscape. The Japanese are proud of their Christian martyrs, and you will see busloads of merry schoolchildren coming not only to

95

view the spot where the bomb fell but also to revere the martyrs who shed their blood for this mysterious man of Galilee, Jesus Christ. Don't miss Nagasaki!

You are coming to Japan to study the new mysticism. And for that I believe Nagasaki is as important as Kyoto. For martyrdom and mysticism are closely allied. In primitive Christianity we hear little about mysticism and much about martyrdom. Is there any connection between the two? I believe there is. For the mystic no less than the martyr faces death and accepts it. The Zen people say that you should sit in meditation as if a samurai was standing in front of you with sword upheld, ready to kill you with a single stroke. In this way you constantly face death. And the time comes when, liberated from the fear of death, you are filled with enlightenment and joy.

And in the same way the Christian mystic must face death just as the Christian martyr faces death. Perhaps authentic mysticism can be called a martyrdom. let me explain.

I don't know if you have read Ernest Becker's prize-winning book *The Denial of Death*. The author claims that the fear of death is very deeply rooted in all human beings, that it lurks behind the sense of insecurity, discouragement, depression, anxiety, neuroses, phobic state, schizophrenia, etc. But, says Becker, most human beings repress the fear of death and walk around as though they are immortal and will never die. In short they deny death. So much for Ernest Becker.

What I want to say is that the mystic who sits or kneels in meditation represses or denies nothing. The whole unconscious life comes to the surface: one is confronted with the inner demons. First one must face one's shadow and accept it. Then comes the void — which is total death. One is face to face with death like the Zen person who sits in front of the samurai's upraised sword. Terrible indeed is this confrontation with death. It is the core of the dark night which can also be called the great death. Yes, one is faced with total death, not only death of one's ego but the death of everything, with nothingness, with emptiness, with the very death of God. Denial is no longer possible. One must embrace death, become one with death. And with this comes a wonderful liberation and a great enlightenment when one cries out with Paul: 'O death, where is thy victory? O death, where is thy sting?' (1 Corinthians 15:55)

96

And of course Jesus lived with death and embraced it. Read the gospel of Luke and you see a Jesus whose eyes were fixed on Jerusalem. Death he feared; but going through that fear in Gethsemane he arrived at a deep peace which never deserted him during his passion. The martyrs, too, faced death and went through their fear, coming to liberation and enlightenment. In this sense they were mystics.

In my last letter I urged you to read *Silence* by Shusaku Endo. And I also said that this novel was, and is, controversial. Endo wrote it in Nagasaki, and while translating I visited Nagasaki and the off-shore islands. I got a rather cool reception from many of the Christians who thought that Endo had been less than fair to their illustrious, martyred ancestors: he seemed to think that martyrdom is not a good idea.

Yet I believe that Endo has the greatest respect for the Japanese martyrs; but he is a modern man who confronts martyrdom in the context of the twentieth century. And is it not clear to everyone that we live in an age of dialogue? The Second Vatican Council was a clarion call to dialogue between religions, between nations and between people in all walks of life. In the hearts of millions the conviction is growing and growing (and may it continue to grow) that problems are not solved by violence and war but by talking and listening and working things out. Compromise is completely necessary. And what about the martyrs? Would it not be better if they could talk, listen, explain, compromise, work things out?

Endo's hero compromises. He tramples on the crucifix in order to save his beloved Christians from further suffering. It is a heart-rending decision, the kind of decision made by thousands who have found themselves in similar circumstance. So painful is the whole thing that, while translating the book, I fell into something like depression and decided I would translate no more books by this author.

Yet *Silence* does not deny the value of martyrdom. It simply underlines the wise words of *Ecclesiastes* that there is a time to live and a time to die. Martyrdom is an act of love; it is based on a choice of love. One must discern (and discernment is a key word in our day) when one is authentically laying down one's life for one's friends, as Jesus laid down his life for us. And if the offering of our life is an authentic act of love, it will be recognized by the modern world. No one questions the goodness and heroism of Maximilian Kolbe who laid down his life for his friend in Auschwitz. No one questions the love and heroism of Edith Stein. No one questions the immense value of the heroic death of Archbishop Romero. We all agree that the six Jesuits and their two companions in El Salvador heroically laid down their lives for social justice in a world torn by oppression.

Let me recommend another book I translated: *The Bells of Nagasaki*. The author, Takashi Nagai, was a doctor who survived the atomic conflagration only to die of leukaemia six years after the war. His book is not only an eye-witness account of the Nagasaki tragedy, it is also the story of a conversion of heart, the story of one who was converted from a total dedication to the Japanese war machine to a total dedication to world peace. What a mystic was Nagai! As he lay dying he kept praying for peace — peace, peace, peace. 'The people of Nagasaki prostrate themselves before God and pray: "Grant that Nagasaki may be the last atomic wilderness in the history of the world."

Like Shusaku Endo, Nagai is a controversial figure — but for a different reason. Whereas Endo seems to downgrade martyrdom, Nagai seems to glorify martyrdom and death as the only way to peace. For him the atomic holocaust was an offering to God, a sacrifice that God demanded for an end to the war. 'The atomic bomb falling on Nagasaki,' he writes, 'was it not a great act of Divine Providence? It was a grace from God. Nagasaki must give thanks to God'. And again :

> Is there not a profound relationship between the destruction of Nagasaki and the end of the war? Nagasaki, the only holy place in all Japan — was it not chosen as a victim, a pure lamb, to be slaughtered and burned on the altar of sacrifice to expiate the sins committed by humanity in the Second World War?

If these were the words of an armchair theologian I'd throw them in the bin. But they were written by one who lost his all in the bomb and now lay dying of leukaemia.

Terrible though it is, Nagai's book did not leave me depressed. I laid it down asking myself if the people who suffered were blessed and the people who caused the suffering were to be pitied.

Now Nagai makes me think of something quite different. I have just heard of the latest IRA atrocity causing the cruel death of innocent people. This war has dragged on for twelve years. How will it end? Is it possible that Nagai was right when he said: 'In order to restore peace to the world it was not sufficient to repent. We had to obtain God's pardon through the offering of a great sacrifice'? And what will be the great sacrifice in Ireland? I tremble to think of that.

I have just returned from London where I spent three weeks in a church in Kensington. I love London. I recall a song we used to sing: 'Oh, I lost my way in a thick, thick fog, in a thick, thick fog in London . . . and at half past two, when the moon broke through, I was all alone with Nelson in Trafalgar Square.' Anyhow I walked to Trafalgar Square and to Hyde Park Corner and down Piccadilly. 'Let's all go down the Strand' was another song. And then Victoria and Westminster Abbey. What a sense of history is there! How I enjoy gazing at the imposing monuments to those scoundrels who built the British Empire! But now London Bridge is falling down, falling down, falling down. The fate of all empires. Fallen, fallen is Babylon the great! Alexander, Julius Caesar, Napoleon, John Bull, Uncle Sam. Who will be next? I'm no prophet but I put my money on Beijing.

Now I'm back in John Bull's other island and soon I'll be leaving. I'll stop off in India and Hong Kong. I'll let you have my addresses later. I always love to see your letters in my mail-box.

Greetings to the children.

Bill T.

99

Dear Brian,

I promised to write you from Belfast, and here I am. I arrived by train from Dublin yesterday. Of course there was a bomb on the tracks and we had to get off at Dundalk, travel by bus to Newry, and then continue by train to Belfast. Yes, infuriating! But compared with the killing and bombing and maiming that's going on, it's small potatoes. I'm staying at a church in the Falls Road, the very church in which I was baptized a thousand years ago. I looked it up in the parish records and there was my name as large as life.

This is provo country. Last night I went for a walk up the Falls Road in the rain. The place was tense, full of soldiers and police with sinister guns and rifles, standing beside armoured cars — or saracens as they are called. As I passed by I saw a young soldier in full battle array crouched in a corner with upraised rifle. Our eyes met; and he smiled and said 'Good evening, father!' With a pang I felt the tragic pathos of the whole situation.

So much has happened since I arrived in this country. The IRA have escalated their war. Last September a bomb exploded at the Royal Marine's School of Music at Deal in Kent, killing ten and injuring twenty-two. Then the German wife of a British soldier was shot. Then two young Australians were gunned down in Holland. These are the IRA atrocities that have hit the headlines; but in Belfast there have also been numerous sectarian murders of Catholics — and harassment and torture by the police and the army. Then there was the uproar about the Irishmen who were gaoled in England for crimes they did not commit — the Guildford four and the Birmingham six.

In the *Irish News* for June 1 I read an article by Sinn Fein president, Gerry Adams. At the funeral of the late cardinal, millions of television viewers had watched him walk devoutly to the altar to receive Holy Communion; and the newspapers had asked how he could reconcile his support for armed struggle with the teachings

100

of his Church. His action in receiving the Eucharist was indeed profoundly symbolical and the newspaper had said that 'for many' it was 'deeply confusing, disturbing and offensive'.

Gerry Adams expresses annoyance at this reference to his private religious practice; and he then goes on to speak about the teaching of his Church on violence. 'The Catholic Church is not a pacifist church,' he writes. 'It accepts and upholds the rights of armies. It upholds the right to engage in armed action.' He speaks of his desire for peace. 'Republicans want an end to all violent conflict. We know at first hand the suffering created by war. We are mindful of all the deaths, all the injured, all the imprisoned. Republicans do not dodge their responsibilities.' But this is a country 'which is partitioned, where over a third of its citizens have been forced to emigrate in the last sixty years, where over a third of those who remain live below the poverty line, where 5 per cent of the population control 80 per cent of the wealth, where a part of the national territory and a sizeable section of its citizens are controlled by the military apparatus of a foreign power and where armed conflict has been raging for twenty years.' He also speaks of the lethal plastic bullets and of Loyalist murder gangs possessing British intelligence files on Irish nationalists. He could have spoken about internment without trial and all kinds of cruel injustices.

As I read Gerry Adam's words I was reminded of the old theology of the just war that I learned as a student before the Council. War could be justified under certain circumstances, particularly if it looked like succeeding. And, of course, war was legitimate as a last resort. Then there was the principle of double effect. The army, we learned, may not *intend* the death of innocent men, women and children; but it could *permit* the death of innocent men and women and children in pursuit of its bloodthirsty aims against enemy soldiers.

What casuistry was there! What appalling drivel! How far we got away from the Gospel! 'But I say to you that hear, love your enemies, do good to those who hate you, bless those who curse you, pray for those who abuse you. To him who strikes you on the cheek, offer the other also; and from him who takes away your cloak do not withhold your coat as well' (Luke 6:27). Didn't the old moral theology get more inspiration from Aristotle than from the Gospel? And it seems that some IRA Catholics — and some people who advise them — are working precisely out of that old theology. 'The Catholic Church is not pacifist.'

It seems to me that we cannot have peace until we throw the old just war theology out of the window and search for something new based on the Gospel. We must listen to Mahatma Gandhi, Martin Luther King, Thomas Merton, Dorothy Day. We need to learn from Buddhism with its great reverence for life — for all life, even the life of animals and plants and our whole planet. We need to learn from the Dalai Lama and the tradition of Tibet. But to elaborate a new moral theology academic excellence is not enough. Much more important is conversion to the Gospel.

Let me here pause to say that the situation in Ireland is by no means unique. Similar circumstances prevail in the Middle East, the Punjab, Sri Lanka, the Philippines, South Africa, and Latin America. Now that the danger of nuclear war between the super-powers has receded we are faced with the equally great danger of terrorism and guerrilla warfare in the whole world. After banning nuclear weapons and chemical weapons can we find some way of banning semtex? We can only do that when we find a solution to the underlying problem.

Of course the underlying problem is justice. There will be no solution until we learn to respect the human dignity of all men and women — and of all peoples.

Gandhi had a genius for discovering non-violent ways to justice. Think of his salt march. And then his long fasts, which shook the world. And he undertook these symbolical actions not from anger but to bring about the conversion of the oppressor. Besides Gandhi there is Daniel O'Connell with his monster meetings. Then there was the People Power of the Philippines. And in recent years we have had wonderful examples of peaceful revolution in Eastern Europe. And the challenge is to find non-violent paths to justice. Let me here suggest two non-violent alternatives.

The first is prayer. When Peter was seized and put in prison 'earnest prayer for him was made to God by the church' (Acts 12:5). And we know what happened. An angel did the job. And is it possible that angels are doing something in Eastern Europe and Russia and China and in the whole world? Never let us underestimate the power of the prayer of intercession. And just as earnest prayer was made for Peter by the church, so earnest prayer

102

has been made for Russia and the whole communist world. And once more has prayer proved mightier than the sword?

But now a new dimension of that prayer has appeared. Whereas the prayer for Peter was made by a tiny group of new Christians, prayer for peace can now be made by all religions joining hands and calling out to God. This was wonderfully demonstrated at Assisi when John Paul invited Jews and Muslims and Hindus and Buddhists to pray in unison for world peace. It was there that John Paul spoke to the world of 'another dimension of peace.' That is to say, peace is not just a question of economies and politics and law-making, however important these may be, but more especially of the grace of God. That is why prayer of intercession is the very basis — 'earnest prayer for him was made to God by the Church.'

But intercessory prayer is not the whole story. I remember once in Japan talking to Enomiya-Lassalle about the troubles in Northern Ireland. He said with a wry smile: 'They should all do Zen!' A joke, yes. But many a true word is spoken is jest. There is a Christian contemplative prayer of just being. One simply sits in the presence of God, aware that one is enveloped in this immense love which fills the universe. No words are necessary. No thinking is necessary. In this contemplative prayer my being becomes being-in-love.

Now we will establish peace not only by doing but also, and more importantly, by being. If more and more people can *be* in the presence of God, if more and more people can allow their being to become being-in-love, if more and more people can let their consciousness expand lovingly to all men and women, to the whole environment and to the limitless universe — if we can experience the enormous power of being-in-love then we will be on the royal road to peace.

As for Zen, you know that it was greatly influenced by the non-action, or *wu-wei* of Taoism. And non-action, in turn leads to non-violence. Instead of taking up arms against a sea of troubles one 'sits' and lets the process take place. Let nature act. Let God act. 'For we know him who said,"Vengeance is mine, I will repay".' (Hebrews 10:30). Surrender to God and leave all to him, working by himself or working through me. So much for prayer.

The second non-violent alternative is dialogue. Who can deny that dialogue is one of the great achievements of the modern world?

Day by day the conviction grows that problems are not solved by knives and guns and bombs and semtex but by sitting around a table and talking. Talk, talk, talk. Listen, listen, listen. And always with sincerity and a desire for authenticity. And how we wish that inter religious dialogue would lead the way and set an example for the world! Anyhow, I advise you to read and reread the section on dialogue at the end of *The Church in the Modern World*.

For the Council speaks of dialogue between all men and women — dialogue within the Church, dialogue between Christians, dialogue with people of other faiths, dialogue with agnostics and atheists. 'For our part, the desire for such dialogue . . . excludes no one . . . We include those who oppress the Church and harass her in manifold ways.'

And I need not tell you that dialogue demands the utmost fidelity to the Gospel precepts of love, trust, forgiveness, perseverance, courage, hope and everything that goes under the name of faith. It is a process that demands blood and tears and sweat and toil. It can be a mystical purification no less painful than the dark night of the soul. What a challenge!

It would be wrong to underestimate the dialogue that is courageously going on in Ireland: between Dublin and Westminster, between Protestants and Catholics, between unionists and loyalists. As yet there is no dialogue with the IRA, but that must come. Our dialogue excludes no one. Isn't this the path to peace?

The Second Vatican Council said wisely that there can be no ecumenism worthy of the name without conversion of heart. And the same holds true for peace. There can be no peace worthy of the name without a conversion to non-violence. And since I am here talking about Ireland let me say that there can be no peace without a conversion not just on the part of the northern Irish — people like myself — but on the part of the whole country and even on the part of the second and third generation Irish abroad. It is no secret that the IRA get emotional and financial support from Irish Americans and, until recently, from Irish Australians. Years ago in Fifth Avenue I was stopped by a somewhat dishevelled young man shaking a money-box and asking for help for the IRA.

Conversion to non-violence! If we go back far enough in history I believe we will find that the Celts were a peace-loving people.

I am thinking of the time when St Colmcille and the rest went out from a land of saints and scholars to evangelize Europe. And even much later there were great prophets like O'Connell (the Liberator and the King of the beggars) and Parnell, who wanted freedom without shedding one drop of English or Irish blood. But, alas, the ideological leadership passed into the hands of others, false prophets like Wolfe Tone and Padraig Pearse. Thanks to these and to the Orange Order ('Ulster will fight and Ulster will be right') the evil spirit of violence entered the Irish psyche and it has yet to be exorcised. How can that be done?

I believe there is still plenty of prayer in Ireland, and this will call down God's grace. I believe there are plenty whose being is being-in-love and who are undergoing a deep conversion. I believe there are serious attempts at dialogue and we can hope that those involved will not give in to discouragement and despair. We know that in the US there is an intelligent, non-violent search for justice based on the so-called MacBride principles. All this can give us grounds for hope.

And yet an unsettling thought sometimes comes to my mind. I translated a book about the atomic bomb called *The Bells of Nagasaki*. Takashi Nagai, who lost his wife and his possessions in the bomb and now lay dying of leukaemia, wrote that the holocaust of Nagasaki was, had to be, offered to God to bring peace to the world and to atone for the sins of the Second World War. I am reminded of that text of scripture which says that 'without the shedding of blood there is no forgiveness of sins' (Hebrews 9:22). And note that in Nagasaki innocent blood was shed. The bomb exploded over the cathedral where hundreds were at prayer; and they were wiped out instantly.

Nagai's point is that suffering is necessary. 'Without the shedding of blood there is no forgiveness of sins.' And, 'Was it not necessary that the Christ should suffer these things and enter into his glory?' (Luke 24:26). Nagai has been criticized for this disturbing theology. But one wonders if it contains some truth. Is suffering necessary? The suffering of the innocent? Will there be some cataclysm like Nagasaki? Is the cross really so powerful that it brings peace in the most desperate situations? We can only wonder at the mysterious ways of God.

*

Time is moving on and on. Now I'm preparing to return to Asia. My heart leaps up at the thought. I leave London at the end of June and fly to Madras where I'll spend a couple of weeks. Last time I was in India I lost all my possessions, including my passport. A good experience, I can assure you; but I hope it won't happen again. From India I fly to Hong Kong and then back to Tokyo.

I look forward to hearing from you. Yes a detailed account of your conversion to non-violence and of your prayers for my conversion.

God bless you and yours.

Bill J.T.

Dear Ayako,

Back in Asia! I arrived in Hong Kong a few days ago and found your letter with the familiar hand-writing. Many thanks! Yes, a lot has happened since I flew out of Narita more than a year ago. It's a different world. And is it a different Japan? I have come to see the international dimension of Nippon, with Toyota and Nissan and Mitsubishi flashed on hoardings all over the world. Money really talks, doesn't it?

Back in Asia I am deeply impressed by the energy and vitality and the seething masses of people. People, people, people. People pouring on and off the Star Ferry that chugs across from Kowloon to Hong Kong. People in their thousands in the streets. A couple of years ago I was in mainland China — and there it was bikes, bikes, rivers of bikes flowing through the streets. Here it is men, women and children buying and selling and rushing to work. And what will happen when Beijing takes over in 1997? It is difficult to see these people knuckling down under a totalitarian regime. No one can deny that the Brits have done a good job in Hong Kong. It is well organized, well run — and the people are well educated. I wonder how they'll take to communism, if communism still exists in 1997.

I came here first in 1951 (yes, I was only a kid!) en route to Japan. What a different world that was! Mao Tse-tung and the Red Army had swept down to Canton and to the very gates of Hong Kong. There they stopped. And Hong Kong, was living from day to day, wondering when the communists would cut the water supply or march in to liberate the city. But nothing happened. And Hong Kong is still, nominally at any rate, under British rule.

In 1987 I had an opportunity to visit mainland China. We went by minibus from Macau down south to the island of Sanchian where Xavier, all alone, yielded up his great spirit to God. For me that trip into China opened up a new world. Before that I had stood at the border looking at the immense land mass and wondering what

107

was happening among the billion people beyond those mysterious mountains. Now I was there. And it was just like the Philippines or Korea or parts of Japan. We were welcomed and treated with hospitality. Of course I spoke no Chinese but I could read many of the ideographs and had some idea of where we were and what was happening.

But what about the Church? The communist government (a couple of their representatives were with us in the minibus) wanted to make Xavier's death site a tourist attraction that would draw pilgrims from all over the world. We met the local clergy and attended their Eucharist. They were fine men, living in heroic poverty, trying to preach the Gospel within the framework permitted by the government.

And Christianity is still alive in China. Just as the Nagaski Christians preserved their faith through centuries of cruel persecution, so thousands of Chinese Christians have kept their allegiance to Christ and to the Gospel. When we came to the island of Sanchian, people from neighbouring islands who had heard of our visit came by boat — whole families in big black boats — to attend the Eucharist. At 3 p.m. many of them were still fasting so that they could receive holy communion. Their simple and sterling faith and their silent poverty reminded me of the people of Nagasaki and the off-shore islands. What a strange thing is faith! It grows and deepens in the midst of persecution: in affluence and luxury it withers and dies.

Of course things have now changed in China. While I was in California in May and June of last year, the student protest erupted in Tiananmen Square and the awful massacre took place. Well I remember (and millions of breathless television viewers remember) that lone young man with upraised hands who stood courageously in front of the long column of tanks. And for six minutes he stopped the Red Army. What heroism! Later, in California, I asked my students to write a paper on the humanity of Jesus, and one student wrote about this lone demonstrator, saying that he was a Christ figure and a martyr. What happened to him? I have heard rumours that he was executed. Human rights organizations have identified him as Wang Weilin. He is already canonized *vox populi*. The people of the world have spoken. His name will live in the annals of Chinese and world history.

And what about the future? Mike Mansfield, former US Ambassador to Japan, kept saying that the next century will be the century of the Pacific. The economic and cultural centre, he maintained, would move from the Atlantic to the Pacific. I always thought he was completely right — until I saw world events of 1989 and 1990 during this sabbatical. Now I see several centres, including an Islamic civilization and culture spread throughout the world and transcending notional boundaries. Things are happening that no futurologist predicted.

But China will be great. And I ask myself about the evangelization of this immense country that holds one-fifth of the world's population. What future does the Gospel have in China?

Xavier believed that the fate of all Asia depended on China. For that reason he left Japan and died on that little island, looking longingly at the Chinese coast. And since his time hundreds, perhaps thousands, of missionaries have struggled with China. I deliberately say 'struggled' because it was an anguishing encounter with an immensely rich and ancient culture and with a proud people who did not easily accept the foreign devil, the southern barbarian, the yellow-haired foreigner. But now as we look back in history no one doubts that the great missionary prophet was Italian. Mateo Ricci (1552 – 1610), the wise man from the West, read and wrote the language, loved the culture, respected the religion and wanted to integrate the Chinese rites into Christianity. He is still honoured in China. When I went into the mainland our communist guide spoke respectfully about Mateo Ricci.

And we now see that in the future, whatever the government, Chinese Christianity must be permitted to go its own way, to forge its own rituals, to build its own theology, always remaining faithful to the Gospel and to the people of God throughout the world. How can this be done?

The ecclesiology of Vatican II gives us an inkling of what is possible. Speaking about union with the eastern church (and here the Council means the Churches of the Middle East and of eastern Europe) the Council says that for many centuries the churches of the East and the West went their own way united in faith – and that in time of disagreement the Roman See acted as moderator. Here are the words of the Council :

For many centuries, the Churches of the East and of the West went their own ways, though a brotherly communion of faith and sacramental life bound them together. If disagreements in belief and discipline arose among them, the Roman See by common consent acted as moderator.

The Council goes on to speak in glowing terms of eastern theology and spirituality and of the ancient ecumenical councils that were held in the East and enriched the universal church. And it makes the striking statement :

To remove any shadow of doubt, then, this sacred Synod solemnly declares that the Churches of the East, while keeping in mind the necessary union of the whole Church, have the power to govern themselves according to their own disciplines, since these are better adapted to foster the good of souls.

Council also speaks of the patriarchal churches some of which owe their origin to the apostles themselves. It says that the eastern patriarch is the bishop who has jurisdiction over all bishops and people in his own territory without prejudice to the primacy of the Roman Pontiff. In this the Catholic patriarch differs from the orthodox patriarch who is first among equals, *primus inter pares*.

Could not all this be relevant to the vision of a Christian China?

Underlying everything I have said is a problem of the greatest magnitude: Church and State. 'Render to Caesar the things that are Caesar's and to God the things that are God's.' It is generally said that Christianity made little progress in China and Japan because the missionaries failed to adapt to the indigenous culture. To some extent this is true. But in my opinion a much more basic reason was that Caesar wanted no outside influence. Caesar wanted to control everything (and this is particularly true of the shogun of Japan) and became afraid when the people rendered to God the things that are God's.

Let me here say that this has been a problem in Christianity since the time of Constantine. Caesar, whether he lives in the Kremlin or the White House or Buckingham Palace, wants to control the Church. And all the Christian denominations — Orthodox, Anglican, Roman Catholic and everyone else — have had their struggle with Caesar. "Render to Caesar the things that are Caesar's and to God the things that are God's." Sometimes they have made unhappy compromises. Sometimes they have made good and happy compromises. Sometimes they have courageously appealed for help like Paul who cried: 'I appeal to Caesar.'

The Second Vatican Council saw from bitter experience that interference from Caesar, however well-meaning, could spell disaster. In the past the Catholic Church had conceded to Caesar some right in the appointment of bishops. Now she said: Never again! The Council declared unequivocally that 'the right of nominating and appointing bishops belongs properly, peculiarly and of itself exclusively to the competent ecclesiastical authority.' Lest there be any misunderstanding she repeated that the desire of the Council was 'that in the future no right or privilege of election, nomination, presentation or designation for the office of bishop be any longer granted to civil authorities.'

Now in China today the situation is complex. The principal reason for the refusal to accept Roman Catholicism is political. The Vatican is a sovereign state with representatives throughout the world and specifically in Taiwan. And while this continues, Beijing will not recognize Rome nor will it permit a foreign government to appoint the bishops within its boundaries.

And inside China some priests and bishops feel that in order to keep the faith alive among their flock they must compromise with Caesar. They work within the framework permitted by the government. Perhaps some of them are like the hero of Endo's *Silence* who trampled on the crucifix out of love for Jesus and out of love for the people.

But even if the political dilemma was solved, the problem of Church and State would not automatically vanish. 'Render to Caesar the things that are Caesar's and to God the things that are God's.' How the Holy Spirit will solve this problem in China I do not know. One thing is certain: the Spirit alone can give the true wisdom that will lead to a solution and to the reconciliation for which we all long.

Enough of China. Soon I'll be in Japan. Many thanks for offering to come to the airport. I look forward to seeing your smiling face and hearing about my friends in Tokyo. I arrive at Narita by JAL flight 01 arriving at 2.30 p.m. If for some reason you cannot make it to the airport, don't worry. I'll get the train to Ueno and then a taxi.

May God bless us all.

Bill J⸻ S. J.